The **Chuckle** Brothers

Fifty years of To Me... To You

To Me... To You! That's the Chuckle Brothers celebrating fifty years on stage! Surely not! Oh yes they are!

Of course, they have not always been The Chuckle Brothers but Paul and Barry Elliott have certainly been entertaining the crowds for half a century as well as decades of television shows which have made them a national treasure.

This is their story, written by Paul with a little "help" from Barry in his own special way. The Chuckle Brothers have been filling theatres and pulling in huge viewing figures for their television shows for a few years now, but it was not always like that.

They know what it is like to entertain the lunchtime crowd in a working men's club where most of the audience are reading the Sunday papers and looking at the clock to see if it is time to go home for their roast dinner.

They know what it is like to be paid off or to be let down by promises that were never kept.

The Chuckle Brothers are all about fun and laughter but

behind the scenes they have endured their personal tragedies as well, as you will see in this book.

But make no mistake this is no tale of woe, it is a celebration of two great guys who love what they do and are loved by those they do it for.

If the gift of making people laugh and giving kids some real fun entertainment is worth a knighthood, then arise Sir Paul and Sir Barry and continue to reign supreme in Chuckle Castle where even the portcullis has a smile on its face.

If you have ever laughed with Paul and Barry, then Fifty years of To Me... To You is something you simply cannot miss.

Enjoy!

The
CHUCKLE
BROTHERS

Fifty years of
TO ME... TO YOU

Paul Chuckle

with Bernard Bale

WORLD'S
FAIR

Published by The World's Fair Limited

First published 2014 by The World's Fair Limited
Chambers Business Centre, Chapel Road, Oldham OL8 4QQ

ISBN 978-0-9927757-2-8

Copyright © Paul Elliott 2014

A CIP catalogue record for this book is available from the British Library.

Cover photo © Lynne Whatmore 2014

Printed and bound in the UK by Short Run Press Limited, Exeter EX2 7LW

This book is dedicated to the memory of our special Mum and Dad, our lovely sister Sheila and our brother and mate Colin.

All, sadly, passed on but never out of our hearts.

Special Acknowledgement

With sincerest thanks to Martin Hughes, our chief television producer for more years than he would care to remember and a man with great vision - ChuckleVision!

Also Special Love and Thanks

To Sue and my kids who put up with me during the months it took me to put this book together.

xxx

Picture Acknowledgements

All photographs are from the author's collection. The author would like to acknowledge the following copyright holders:

Section One
Page 4, bottom © Sheffield Newspapers Ltd

Section Two
Page 2, top © Brian Tarr
www.briantarr.co.uk
Page 11, bottom and Page 12 © Jean Havilland
www.jeanhavillandphotography.co.uk
Page 13, bottom by kind permission of Phil Dale for Qdos and Frank Donovan
www.qdosentertainment.co.uk

Contents

Foreword
by Ken Dodd

A Chuckle a Day Keeps the Doctor Away!

I do like a chuckle first thing in the morning and regular chuckles throughout the day with a very special late night chuckle just before I fall asleep. I have even been known to have a chuckle in my sleep. They can't touch you for it because they don't know what you are thinking while you are having a quick chuckle between snores.

Of course there is only one thing better than *having* a chuckle and that is *being* a Chuckle. Paul and Barry have been the Chuckle Brothers for quite a long time now and made millions of people of all ages laugh their socks off. They have made a great contribution to the health service, for as you know, *"A Chuckle a Day Keeps the Doctor Away!"*

The boys come from a great family heritage of entertainers and many theatres have rocked with laughter because of their father and their brothers and, of course, themselves.

They have done it all, television, working men's clubs, theatres. Talking of working men's clubs, I wonder if anyone has gone on stage and asked: "If you are all working men, what are you doing here?"

The Chuckle Brothers are what real entertainment is all about. They sing, they dance, they act and they are very, very funny both visually and vocally. That is real show business because they do all that and keep well within the boundaries of proper family entertainment. You can take your youngest child or your oldest granny and they will all have a great time.

The *ChuckleVision* TV shows should be on the school curriculum because they are just great fun and prove that you can have fun without pressing buttons, swearing or insulting people.

I always want to see people going to the theatre, it is such a magical experience when you go to a panto or a variety show and have some really good laughs. Nobody does that better than the Chuckle Brothers so if you see them advertised, don't hesitate – get your tickets straight away. You won't regret it and you will feel so much better. The Chuckle Brothers will ease your tired chuckle muscles – they might even make your corns feel better!

Happiness and Chuckles Forever

Ken Dodd

Introduction

To Me… To You! Would you believe it's fifty years since Barry and I started out in show business? It isn't! It is! It isn't! It is! Is it?

Even we are amazed when we look back and see how far we have come and how many miles we have travelled, as well as how many performances we have done. I don't think we dare think about that too much, it might frighten us! We have been blessed with being pretty active all our lives and I think that's why we can still sing and dance with the best of them and still make people laugh – and have a lot of laughs ourselves.

Although we were born into a show business environment, it was not automatic that we went into the business ourselves. We tried other jobs but we kept coming back to show business and making people laugh. It is what we did – and hopefully still do – best. It was what made us happy just as it had made our Dad happy and the rest of our family happy. So, you see, the Chuckle Brothers are all his fault.

We are planning to go on for a long time yet so this is only half-time and hopefully there will be another fifty years to write about in 2064. I wonder if England will have won the World Cup again by then or if Rotherham will win the Champions League?

We have had lots of people ask when we were going to write a book about our lives and how we became the Chuckle Brothers.

We kept saying that we didn't think we had done enough yet. The trouble is that you suddenly realise that compared to a lot of people who have written their stories we had actually done quite a lot. So, I set about making notes, with Barry telling me the bits I had got wrong.

Because we keep pretty busy with theatre shows, pantomimes and recordings I couldn't just sit down and write a book. I had to keep writing bits of it, sometimes in the dressing room, sometimes in our camper van, sometimes in my garden at home or on a train and whenever I found the chance.

I am not a serious writer of course, I am a comedy entertainer who can sing and dance a bit so even though I have been told that my writing was pretty good, it still needed editing properly. Enter Bernard Bale who has written loads of books as well as being a journalist, script writer and general wordsmith, the sort of person you can go off very quickly because he knows about punctuation and things like that. He was quite complimentary really but still pointed out the mistakes. So there was Barry on one side, Bernard on the other and me, the real writer, in the middle! The result is this book and I am really pleased that it has finally escaped.

So thanks to the publishers, thanks to our Mum and Dad for having us… Hang on a minute, it's starting to sound as if I have won an Oscar!! Well, perhaps not an Oscar but maybe some other award? No! Not one of those, I know what you are thinking!!

Anyway, thanks to everyone who has followed our careers, switched on the telly to watch us, come to the theatre to see us and has taken the trouble to get this book, which really is not just To Me… To You, but also From Me To You."

All the best

Paul

Chapter 1

Buckets and Spades – and Red Indian Raids

So there we were, standing in almost darkness, just enough light to see each other and we could hear the most marvellous noise an entertainer can ever hope to hear – the excited sounds of a full house of kids with their mums and dads. In just a few moments the house lights would fade, the music would start, the curtains would glide apart and the stage lights would flash into our eyes as a great cheer would erupt from the audience. Total magic!

But for that moment it was peaceful. Barry and I looked at each other and burst out laughing. No, our flies weren't undone, it's just that we were enjoying ourselves, loving every minute of being the Chuckle Brothers. Without saying a single word we both knew that at that moment we were thinking how lucky we were to be going out to meet a fantastic audience. It hadn't always been like that but it was now. Our dreams had come true and we had thousands of pals all over the country who had taken the trouble to come and see us at the theatre.

We have been in this business for fifty years now – yes, 2013 was our anniversary in show business. It's hard to believe because the time goes so quickly and we look so young – well one of us does anyway! Because our audiences are mostly young we are still like big kids ourselves and it's great. Having been entertaining for half a century doesn't really register unless we really think about it, so perhaps that's what we should do, think about it.

How did it start? A lot of people have asked that so let's go back to the beginning when the Chuckles were just a smile.

Our Dad was good at smiling and he was even better at making other people smile because really the Chuckle Brothers are all his fault. He was a comedian, you see, and a very good one who knew the business well even though he was once banned from BBC radio for two years for ending a gag with the line "as smooth as a baby's bottom"! In his later years Dad would often Tut! Tut! at the things some comics got away with in their material on the telly. The things comics say now would have Dad spinning in his grave.

Anyway, our Dad's working life dated back to just after the First World War when he was thirteen years old and took a job down the pit. All his mates from Hetton-le-Hole in County Durham did the same as there was no work unless you went down the coal mine. Don't you think Hetton-le-Hole is a great name for the place where miners live?!

Down the mines, like in factories and other workplaces, there was always a lot of banter and Dad spent the whole day making all the guys down the pit laugh with his gags and impersonations. It backfired on him though because one day the foreman called him in and told him – through tears of laughter – that he would have to go as no one was getting any coal out while he was keeping up the gags. I don't think the foreman wanted to let him go but he had little choice as no work was getting done. He did make a suggestion though which was to make a big difference to our lives and we weren't even around then. When he told our Dad the bad news he added: "Why don't you try out with the Carrol Levis talent show at the local theatre on Monday night? I'm sure they'll love you."

Dad thought about it. The only family member who had had anything to do with show business was his uncle – our great uncle of course – who was a magician with the stage name of Patton. So Dad called himself Gene Patton and went along for the talent show. What do you mean, who was Carrol Levis? He was a star in his own right in those days. He was the Hughie Green of his time. Hughie Green? Oh all right. Hughie Green was the Simon Cowell of his time.

So Dad went along to appear on the show and the foreman was dead right. Dad stormed them and made it through to the final on the Saturday night. That's how it worked in those days. Carrol Levis brought his talent show to town for a week with local talent and a couple of his own regulars on stage every night, with the big final on the Saturday. The theatres used to be packed.

The local paper had been in and reported how funny this young man named Gene Patton was and told their readers they ought to go along and see him. Carrol Levis was thrilled to bits of course, especially with the House Full signs outside the theatre for the Saturday night final. Well, Dad did it again and brought the house down. He won and collected his two pounds prize. Imagine that, two pounds! He was delighted of course and all the more when Carrol Levis offered him the chance to tour with him as one of his regulars.

Dad accepted of course and off he went. Dad would perform in the talent contest on the Monday, get the press and then win the Saturday final, it was a great job for his first year in show business and he turned professional after that and never looked back. We've had times of not looking back as well but for different reasons.

He earned a good reputation for himself and toured the country in revues, music hall and variety shows. It was all live entertainment in those days as television didn't really take off until he retired in 1954, although he did quite a few radio broadcasts, especially on Radio North. On stage, though, he certainly learned the trade and became a much-loved entertainer who knew how to give his audiences the best and get the best out of them.

Like a lot of entertainers, his career was interrupted by the Second World War. He was now father of our four older siblings, Jimmy, Brian, Sheila and Colin but he enlisted in the RAF where he became a small arms instructor – it was the arms that were small, not him. The camp where he was stationed had no entertainment at all so he decided to create a show using the talents of conscripts. He named it 'Rafadrome' and the show was such a huge success that his commanding officer invited some top brass from London to see it. They loved it too, so Dad found himself providing shows to entertain the troops for the rest of the war. Must have frightened the life out of Hitler!

During the war, someone had another bright idea which turned out to work really well. It was in 1943 that the 'Gang Show' was born to entertain the lads fighting in India and Burma and guess who was given command of one of those units – our Dad! They were much-loved shows too and a fair bit of talent came out of them.

One young drummer with the party in India turned out to be a very funny guy and a great help to Dad. The lad was only nineteen at the time but as well as being pretty hot on the drums he turned out to be a great stooge and could pull all sorts of faces and do all sorts of voices and accents in the various sketches. It was a quite a milestone in the career of the great Peter Sellers.

In April 1944, after a bit of leave, Dad was sent out with a concert party to India once again. Mum waved him goodbye and prepared to say hello to someone new. No, not what you are thinking. The 'someone new' was another baby on the way. Yes, she was pregnant for the fifth time. I'm not sure if the world was ready for this but on December 24th of that year the baby was born. All babies are beautiful except this one. That's right, it was Barry!

Barry was born on Christmas Eve 1944 and I think the rest of the family would sooner have had an orange or a walnut. Mind you, he probably looked like both. He was born at home in Meadow Street, Masborough, Rotherham in the middle of an air raid on Sheffield. Our brothers Jim, Bri, Col and our sister She were all upstairs watching the firework display which was the falling of bombs. We have not discovered if it was true that the Luftwaffe waved white flags when they heard him yell for the first time, but that was the last ever air raid on Sheffield. To this day on December 24th a V sign appears on Barry's forehead, which is very off-putting when you are on stage with him during a pantomime!

After the war finally ended Dad went straight back to working on touring shows. Mum and he needed the income as there were now five children to feed. In some ways it was a shame that he had to get on with it because Peter Seller's mum wanted Dad to wait for Peter to be demobbed so she could set them up in a show in London's West End. Unfortunately it would have been another six months because of Peter's age. He had to stay in the RAF for a bit longer as he was only twenty and had to finish National Service.

Dad couldn't afford to wait as they needed the money and the first job he was offered was a twelve-month touring show which meant regular income for the whole year. It was quite normal in those days for the same show to tour for a year or more as there were so many theatres around the UK that you could probably tour for three years without going back to the same theatre. Remember that shows appeared in a theatre for a whole week then. That doesn't happen now, more's the pity.

Acts like the legendary Wilson, Kepple and Betty and their very famous Sand Dance act topped the bill for many years with just one routine. They didn't need to change their material as it was a long time between going back to the same town. Had they been around today, people would see the act on TV and that would be it. Still, they were brilliant and not many people know this, but they had five or six different 'Betty' girls in the act over the years. Once the young lady passed the age of 22 or 23 they would take on a new Betty aged about eighteen. I'm not sure if they would get away with that now.

Another story about them, which incidentally was related to us by HRH Princess Margaret (name dropper!) when we appeared in a Children's Royal Variety Performance, was when Wilson, Kepple and Betty were booked to work in Las Vegas in the 1950s they took their own sand with them for the act. Customs were not amused at this as Las Vegas is in the middle of a desert and they have plenty of sand of their own!

Are you ready for this next bit? Sit down to read this but my own big moment came in October 1947 when I was introduced to the world. I don't think the world was too impressed but it meant a lot to me. I didn't make a big showbizzy entrance like Barry, who had air raid sirens and the sky being lit up to celebrate his arrival. No, none of that for me. All I got, so I am told, was my sister shouting down the stairs: "What is it?" The answer came back from a typically pro house: "It's a baby!"

Once she got the real answer that she had a lovely – yes, lovely! – baby brother she turned round and went back to her room as she was so disappointed that it wasn't a sister. She felt that she had enough brothers already. Apparently she stayed in her room for ages, well three minutes anyway. Then she couldn't resist taking a look at me, well, who could?

Her disappointment quickly faded and she really looked after all of us all. She is sorely missed by all of us as she passed away on my birthday in 2006 because of that awful cancer thing. Sheila believed, as I do, that she will still be there now watching me write this. Big kiss She X.

When Barry was three years old and I was around five months – I like to remind him of that although he reminds me of his being the older brother too – the family moved to a new house in Lockwood Close, East Herringthorpe, Rotherham. Only Yorkshire could have an East Herringthorpe. I have lots of fond memories of that house and street. Lots of new families moved in there at the same time as us, which meant that with fifteen houses in the street there were five lads, including me, within two months of each other and growing up together. It was really fabulous and we had a lot of fun. I often think back to all the games we got up to.

Mostly we were into football of course, although we did play cricket in the summer. Barry also had five mates the same age and there were a few lads in between, plus a few older, so you can imagine that our football and other games were quite involved. There were three girls too, which was fine while we were kids but not so good when we grew to THAT age. My closest pal was Philip Cliff.

From an early age we all did everything together, mostly football in our back garden, which was the biggest in the street. Council houses always have decent sized gardens but ours was extra large. We played all sorts of games there – it was like an Olympic stadium to us. I vividly remember some of the things we did which, looking back, sound extraordinary compared with today.

As an example, we did human show jumping. We'd been watching the Horse of the Year Show on the telly and went straight outside and built a course of fences – some higher, some wider. I can see us all now prancing around like horses, jumping the fences, trying not to knock any down and picking up four faults if we did. It was great. Must do that again sometime. You know, we never had a refusal!

Another time we'd been to watch the motorbike scrambling at the top of our estate and next day we set up a scrambling track for our push bikes. It's a good job that Mum and Dad weren't keen gardeners! I know it sounds like old farts time but kids don't seem to have fun like that any more what with all the computer things they have. That's a shame really because of all the fresh air we had. I'm sure, having brought up four boys myself, that kids would benefit by doing what we did. It won't happen, I know, but what a shame.

We'd set up the garden with goals at each end – we even tried to make nets with string once, I seem to recall, but one shot and the ball went straight through them. Still, it was fun making them and as well as the exercise we had to use our brains to create those nets. It is not a reflection of our brains that they didn't work. We used to play matches against teams from Haywood Close down the hill. There were a lot more kids of our age at that time.

A few years after the Second World War the nation was asked to produce as many offspring as possible and it became known, I think, as the baby boom. Can you imagine that now? Imagine the Prime Minister make a television broadcast and telling the nation: "We would like you to do a lot more... that is to say, we would like you to... er, the government thinks it might be a good idea for you to spend more time in the bedroom and create families." The contraception industry would be up in arms. Now there's a thought!

Anyway, moving on, the lads from Haywood Close were a bit harder than us. Our street seemed to be a bit posher, or so we thought at the time. One of our lads even had a handkerchief – for weeks. We used to get a kicking sometimes but we always beat them. Those are among many great memories – like sleeping in a tent on warm summer nights.

Mind you, that was a bit eerie once. It was pitch black dark and totally silent apart from an owl with a sense of humour who kept Woo Wooing to make us jump and keep us awake. I can't properly remember who was in the tent but it was probably Mick Churm, a very good mate from number 1 and the eldest of us all. Sandy Williams was probably another. He lived next door at number 9 and was a couple of weeks older than me. He was the only one who didn't go to our school as his family were Catholics and had their own school. Phil Cliff was probably in the tent as well. He lived two doors away at number 6.

So, there we were in the tent and getting a bit spooked. We were determined and sat it out for what seemed an age. None of us could get to sleep. I reckon we must have been eight or nine years old at the time, so pretty young to be out in the wilderness with all the wild animals and such around. What about the mad axeman from number 4!

Just as he came to mind we heard footsteps coming slowly

through the grass. We held our breath as the footsteps stopped outside the tent. We all froze with eyes wide open, not knowing whether to turn on our torches or not. Slowly the tent ties were being unfastened.

Have you ever felt scared, really scared? Well, I'd never felt so frightened in all my young life! But then Mrs Cliff stuck her head into the tent and asked if we were all okay and does Philip want to come home to his nice warm bed. There was no way Phil was going to up and leave his mates, but he did. We stayed there and eventually dropped off to sleep until waking up at five o'clock in the morning with the birds singing to us. None of us had ever seen five in the morning before so it was really cool. The air was so fresh and the sun was up over the hill and it felt very warm on our faces. What a lovely way to wake up.

That summer's day was superb and went on forever. We slept in the tent the following night too, but this time Phil stayed the whole night as well and first thing in the morning we took some bottles back to the shop on Badsley Moor Lane and got 2d (remember those) back on each one, which meant that we could buy our own breakfasts. We got loads of penny rolls and chews and things. You could get four chews for 1d.

Okay, let's stop for a moment and explain to those who are pretending not to know. A 'd' was a penny. You got twelve of them for a shilling and twenty shillings to the pound so 240 pennies to the pound. Half a crown was two shillings and sixpence, and ten bob was something we never had! Simple, wasn't it, not like now when you get 100 pennies to the pound. That is so confusing!

The summer also means holidays of course. Well, I say "of course" but the truth is we didn't really get holidays actually away at the seaside and going abroad for holidays was something you never heard of. It was exciting enough to see a plane, let alone think of actually going on one. Still, we did have a one-day holiday now and then. Yes, that's right we were day-trippers long before The Beatles started singing about it. Most years the highlight of the holiday season was a charabanc trip to Cleethorpes, organised by Dad's working men's club.

They were great days out and the days always seemed much longer then. The first part of the adventure was getting down to All Saints Square in Rotherham for about half past six in the morning. We didn't need telling twice to get up. I would have gone to bed dressed and with my shoes on if I could have got away with it. It was so exciting that sleep was almost out of the question. There was even excitement about whether we would be going in a new bus or an old one. It didn't really matter because as long as it got to us and then got to Cleethorpes, who cared? We always wanted the back seats or the front seats and if we got either we were always thrilled to bits.

The bus would leave at seven o'clock and if there were any latecomers they would really get a lot of stick from everyone. After about an hour the "charra" would stop at a cafe for a toilet break. Mums would get tea organised and the kids would have crisps and pop. In those days this was about halfway but today you can get from Rotherham to Cleethorpes in about an hour with no road works, traffic jams and with a following wind, if you'll pardon the thought.

The total excitement when we arrived at last at the coast was something else. We all wanted to be the first to see the sea but you could smell it before you saw it, so totally different from the air we breathed in at home where the coal mines and the steel works of South Yorkshire produced an atmosphere all of their own.

I remember going to school on a foggy morning with a scarf wrapped round my face, looking like a young bandit. You literally could not see more than ten feet in front of you and crossing Valley Road at the bottom of our hill was petrifying! You had to stand and listen to hear where the traffic was because you couldn't see it. If you thought it was fairly safe you used to have to run for your life across the road. I suppose unless you lived at that time you would not believe how sort of orange-grey the smog was. Thankfully that's a thing of the past with smokeless fuels nowadays and the only time you get a fog like that is if Barry tries to dry his socks in the microwave!

Where were we? Oh yes, the day out in Cleethorpes. Well, when we got there the first thing we did was to go straight to the beach with our buckets and spades, which we had kept in great condition from the year before. They were our special link to the seaside so they were kept almost like trophies. Then it was off with our shoes and socks and in for a paddle.

I clearly remember a boy at the side of me with the filthiest feet you've ever seen. They were "black bright" as they say in Yorkshire. I just had to say something so I stated the obvious: "Your feet are dirty, aren't they?" Without hesitation he replied: "Well, we didn't come here last year."

We never bothered with food or anything like that at that time of the day, we just wanted the beach and on one occasion we were so caught up in building the biggest sandcastle ever that we didn't see the tide coming in. For those of you who don't know Cleethorpes (probably most of you actually), the tide goes out so far you can hardly see the sea. The sand is so flat I think it goes out almost a mile. Don't quote me on that but it is a very, very long way. They say that on a clear day you can see the sea. Just a joke, we still like Cleethorpes.

So there we were creating a massive sandcastle masterpiece of classic architecture when somebody noticed that the sea had come in and was all around us. It was a bit like that scene in *Chitty Chitty Bang Bang* but with a bit more of a sand bank. We had no idea how deep the water was between us and the beach but a big lad who was about twelve led the way and we all followed on in single file. We were a little bit worried when the water came above his waist as he was at least a foot taller than us little 'uns but we all braved it, as you did in those days, and waded on though the sea water came up to our chests. We got through, which was a good job really because minutes later where we were standing was about eight feet under water. We were safe! More importantly our buckets and spades were safe too and would survive for next year's trip. Great times.

Of course we always hated it when we all had to make our way back to the bus at around half past five, ready for the journey home. It was fun when we stopped at a country pub on the return journey though. The mums and dads were all inside with their pints and us kids were in the car park with, yes, you guessed it, our crisps and pop. Many a time we had to have seconds as it was difficult to get parents out of the pub. Well, it was a club outing for them too. We really slept when we got home, I can tell you.

On one trip to Cleethorpes the oldies were in a drinking establishment before returning to the coach and they met up with one of the guys off our estate back in East Herringthorpe. He'd had far too much to drink and was on the verge of passing out so a few of the dads helped him back to the bus and laid him down on the back seat to help him sleep it off on the way home. When he was awakened to get off the coach back home in Rotherham he said: "Where's me wife and kids?"

It turned out that he wasn't on the trip but was on a fortnight's holiday with his family in Cleethorpes and had only been there two days. I've no idea how he got back to them or what sort of reception he got when he rejoined them. There were no mobile phones back then so he had no way of telling his wife what had happened until he actually met up with them again. Hope the hangover was worth it!

We did get some holidays as well as the day trips. We thought we were dead lucky when our older brothers Jimmy and Brian landed themselves a summer season because that meant we could go and have a couple of weeks with them at the seaside. We thought they would be delighted to have us around to remind them of home!

My earliest recollection was of them doing a season in Rhyl in North Wales, so we were able to have a fortnight's holiday 'abroad'. Rhyl is quite a nice place and in the 1950s it was really vibrant and I still get excited when I think about the penny arcades, the boating lake, the beach, the chippies and, of course, the theatres. Jimmy and Brian were appearing in a show called *Quaintesques* at the Ampitheatre. Can you imagine calling a show Quaintesques these days? It sounds like a batch of Mr Kipling cakes with different colour icing. Would you like a bone china cup of tea and a Quaintesque or two? Sorry, I was getting carried away.

Anyway, we went on holiday with them and while I am sure Rhyl had its fair share of rain, I honestly don't remember any. It was sunshine all the way for us. We loved going to the big open air swimming pool. It wasn't just going swimming but watching a show with the Crazy Diving Team. We loved them with all their silly dives which made us laugh but also made us think better them than us!

You know, I think everyone should do this at some time in their lives – not the crazy diving, writing down the things of your past. It's amazing the things that come back to you, things you thought you'd forgotten. At Rhyl, for instance, we liked being on the paddle boats. Our legs were like jelly afterwards but then we liked jelly so it didn't matter. We used to become world champion golfers on the putting green and of course, we were cowboy heroes on the donkeys. That's one thing you still see at a lot of seaside resorts – donkey rides. Perhaps you don't see as many as there used to be but the traditional still exists and kids still love to ride them, or at least their parents and grandparents like to see the kids ride them even if the kids themselves aren't too sure.

Barry and I loved them though and I can remember our Mum going up to a man who was holding onto some donkeys on the beach. "Can you hire these donkeys?" she asked.

"Yes love, there's a little screw just under the saddle," he instantly replied. Barry and I were a bit worried about that as like most kids we were literalists and took everyone's word for everything. If Mum or Dad said: "You'll smile on the other side of your face in a minute," Barry and I stared at each other to see if our mouths were going to move to the backs of our heads.

Another summer we went back to dear old Cleethorpes for a full two weeks holiday as Dad was doing a summer season there. That's where I broke Barry's two front teeth! We stayed in a caravan on a site and were playing Cowboys and Indians, as all young lads did in those days.

Barry had lost his gun and we were pinned down by the Indians. There was only him and me against our imaginary enemy. At the height of the siege I spotted Barry's gun and I thought I would throw it to him. He was hiding behind a water stand and I was shielding behind a caravan. The imaginary arrows were flying at us from all directions and there were some pretty near misses, I can tell you.

I threw the gun to Barry and shouted: "Here's your gun Baz!" He looked out and shouted "What?" just as the gun hit the tarmac, bounced up and smacked him straight in the mouth.

The battle suddenly came to a halt as Barry ran in to Mum, holding his hand to his mouth. I daren't go in for ages, thinking I would be in real trouble. Mum and Barry recognised that it was an accident so there were no hard feelings – well not for me anyway but then I hadn't just been hit in the mouth with a metal gun! Maybe that's why I was often called a loose cannon!

Barry was okay about it, although he wasn't too happy when we got back to Rotherham and he had to go to the dentist to have his broken teeth drilled. They didn't numb your gum in the 1950s, not at our dentist anyway and Barry nearly went through the roof with pain. After that I refused to have a filling, although a very good friend of mine, Richard Joseph, is a dentist. I have nothing against dentists as long as they leave my mouth alone!

All summers were fabulous when we were kids. The garden would become a cricket ground with six and out over the fence. You'd get some great spin on the wicket as the ball bounced off a clump of grass. In the evening we would play on the street with the gas lamp (renamed the lamp post when they turned it into electric, although when I was young it was powered by gas and the man would walk round the estate with his long stick and pull the lever to light up the lamp). The gas lamp was not only our floodlight but sometimes became the wicket too.

It wasn't all high days and holidays when we were kids. We went to school as well, something we had to do rather than wanted or liked to do. I remember starting at Badsley Moor Lane Infant School when I was five years old. Mick Churm called for me with his mum and off we went. I was fine until Mum left then I too wanted to leave. However the delights of the sandpit and playing with water soon distracted me. Infant school was not bad really. We had some great toys to play with, the likes of which none of us from the Close had ever seen before. There were pedal cars and the like and us infants were easily led into actually liking school.

I wonder how many of you remember the school milk? I never liked it but we had to drink it every morning at playtime. In the summer it was all creamy and warm and in the winter it was almost frozen solid. The milk monitor would bring the milk in and put it on the radiator which made it creamy and warm again. Yuk!

I also never liked school dinners. I only stayed just the once. Mum had paid for the week so she made me get our money's worth but my stomach still churns every time I think of it. The whole school would reek of over-boiled cabbage whatever the dinner was. There might not have been a cabbage for miles but the dinner always still smelled of cabbage!

We had one and a half hours for dinner so Phil and I would run all the way home, about a mile only it seemed like three miles when you're little. We would get our dinner down quickly and then play football for half an hour before galloping back to school. The times we charged breathlessly through the iron gate just as the bell was ringing and the panics we caused ourselves in getting in line before the last kids went in. The clanging of the bell was more like an alarm than a school bell.

We did the same thing at the senior school, Spurley Hey. The difference there was that if you were late three times in a week you would get the cane. It wasn't very nice but it kept everyone in check. Even the hardest of lads in class who were always in trouble didn't like getting the cane. They would stand at the front of the class with tears in their eyes, holding out their hands very flat as they had been told to keep their thumbs out of the way. Suddenly there was a swish and a thwack! They tried not to cry but didn't do a very good job of it. Yes, it was barbaric but it stopped the rest of the class doing the same thing. Now it seems anything goes at school and this seems to spill over after they leave school too and start drinking. Do you know, I can feel a bit of the grumpy old man coming on again, so I'll leave it there.

The best part of school was football and cricket of course. If that was all you had to do at school I would have loved every minute of it. I remember my first few weeks at Spurley and being mortified that I couldn't get in the school team because I was too small. I didn't actually grow very much until I was seventeen.

The team was coached by a teacher called Brian Copley who took us for geography. I didn't do very well at geography in those days and regularly came 22nd or 23rd out of 25, a pity really because I'm quite good at it now, especially in the UK after all the travelling we have done from theatre to theatre. Back to the football and the school team wasn't doing very well and Mr Copley decided that there must be some hidden talent in the school so he organised a trial. I was excited when I heard about it because I thought it was going to be my big moment to prove everyone that I was a soccer star even if I wasn't very big.

The trial was at one o'clock before starting afternoon lessons. I shot out of school at noon as usual, ran up the hill to the bus stop on Doncaster Road to catch the 12.05pm bus. I got off at the usual bus stop, sprinted home and I was there in about twenty minutes from sprinting out of the school gate. I wolfed down dinner, grabbed my football boots and shot back to the bus stop. By 12.55pm I was back at school and had amazed myself by how I had managed to get all that done in just 55 minutes.

I loved every minute of that trial and I played really well even though I thought I had blown it when I missed the goal with only the goalie to beat after leaving defenders in my wake. The trouble was that my left foot was useless but I didn't want the teacher to know that so I just hit the ball with my right. The ball just bobbled and bounced and slowly found its way into the arms of the grateful goalie, my pal for many years after, John Brownrigg.

I thought I had blown my chances and I was pretty fed up as we changed and went off to maths or something just as dreary. I could not have been more wrong. When the team went up on the notice board for the next school game I didn't bother looking until Mick C came running up to me and dragged me to look at it. There at No 4 was Elliott! Me! I was in the school team! I had actually made it! Wow!

After that I was in the team right through to getting badly injured a couple of years later. What a team we were. Most of us were not very big but we made up for it with skill. Our centre forward William Slack – amazing how these memories keep flooding back – was different from the rest of us. He was 6ft tall at age twelve and was also a superb swimmer who not only competed for the school but also for the town and the county.

I was moved in the second year up to right wing as I had a lot of speed in those days. It was great crossing the ball for Will as you knew he would always be on the end of it if you dropped it on the penalty spot. Centre halves would jump as high as they could but still didn't get up to his height and the ball ended up in the back of the net 90 per cent of the time. No wonder we went unbeaten for two years!

Our pal Phil was always the class player on the pitch and even at eight years old when the big lads and the men would play 15-a-side (and sometimes 20-a-side) he would be invited to play because he was that good.

He left school at fifteen, as I did, and to my disgust he joined Sheffield United as an apprentice. My disgust was because from the age of eight Phil and I would get the bus every Saturday to Rotherham and walk the rest of the way to Millmoor at Masbrough for the game. One week it would be the first team and the next week the reserves but we were always there and I was and always have been a Miller through and through.

I was appalled that he joined Sheffield United because Rotherham wanted him and he could have joined them but his dad said he would have a better career at Bramall Lane. He could even have joined Leeds United because they also wanted him but he would have had to have left home for that and he loved the house on Lockwood Close too much.

I can picture him now walking up the Close at lunchtime, dragging his kit bag and looking half dead after a training session. Professional football isn't as easy as you might think. Still, Phil got the career which we both dreamed of as kids. He was with the Blades until he was 21 and then joined Chesterfield where he became something of an icon, finally ending his career with Worksop Town. Phil had been there and got the tee-shirt as they say. Lucky sod.

As for Barry and me, well, work beckoned and neither of us were that keen. Barry was ahead of me of course, being that little bit older. Had we known what was in store, I think we might have allowed ourselves a "chuckle" or two.

Chapter 2

Heigh-ho, Heigh-ho – It's Off to Work We Go!

Now and then Barry likes to remind me that he is older than me. There are times I like to remind him that I am younger than him. The fact that there's a couple of years difference doesn't mean very much now, but it did when we were teenagers.

Barry left school when he was fifteen, in December 1959. I also left when I was fifteen but that was three years later. I envied him leaving but made the best of it. Barry had always dreamed of going into show business but even with family connections it was never that easy. We came from an age when you had to be able to actually do something, not just stand there looking pretty.

Well, we all wondered what Barry might do when he left school but in fact he landed on his feet because in December

1960 he joined a boy band – yes we had them in those days too – called Monty Sidford's Singing Scholars. Barry could sing but he was never a great scholar so I was a bit surprised that he got the job!

One of them played the piano and the others sang all kinds of harmonies. They were really good, too. Freddie Starr was in the singing group for about six weeks until he was asked to leave for being a crackpot.

Barry had a great time. They toured Germany and then did a summer season at Ramsgate which was really good because I was allowed to go and stay with him for a couple of weeks during the school holidays. I enjoyed that because I didn't know the south coast at all and we were able to explore Ramsgate and Margate during the day and then I could sample the atmosphere of the show when Barry was working.

Sadly the Scholars broke up at the end of 1960 and Barry had to think about getting a "proper job". He came home and thought about it but not for long because he quickly put together an act as a solo comedian – these days it is known as being a stand-up comedian which I have always found a bit odd because you don't see many comedians lying down to do their act!

Anyway, Barry started getting work and spent the next two years appearing at working men's clubs. It wasn't enough to call it a career though and most entertainers who did those clubs had other work as well. Barry was no exception and he did get that proper job to keep him going during the week, with his comedy engagements mostly at weekends.

Barry actually worked for the British Oxygen Company in the same office as another entertainer you might have heard of – Tony Christie. They often worked together at the same clubs at weekends. Tony eventually found the way to Amarillo and Barry found the way to Mablethorpe.

During this time I was growing up and getting through my school years so that by the time I left in December 1962 I was ready to tread the same road as my older brothers. Guess what happened – nothing! Barry and I rehearsed a comedy act together but January came and went and nothing happened. February came and went and nothing happened. It was starting to look as if I might have to sniff out a job at British Oxygen too until a call came and we were booked for an engagement at the Palladium. Yes, the Palladium!

It was actually the Palladium, Edinburgh and we were to open the show with a song and dance routine. Dorothy Squires was top of the bill so it was all very exciting, working with a star and going to a foreign country – Scotland – for my first booking. Stardom was within easy reach! Not really, but the dream was still real.

I remember our Mum putting us on the train at Rotherham Masborough station. She bought the tickets for us which meant that we owed her £3 each. She wasn't mean about money but wanted us to learn to stand on our own two feet right from the start. Our 'digs' were arranged and were going to cost us £2.10s, or £2.50p in today's money. Considering that we were only getting £10 between us for the week we were not going to make much money but the experience was well worth it.

We had been backstage dozens of times before when we went to see our Dad and also our older brothers Jimmy and Brian – the Patton Brothers – as well as our sister, Sheila, who had been a dancer for a couple of years.

It's funny that we had spent many of our younger years in dressing rooms with women semi-undressed and getting changed. That never meant anything to us, it was just part of the natural way of life and we kind of thought everyone lived that way. Of course, Barry had his experience with the Scholars so it was not all new to us but it is different when you are going on stage yourself.

We have always loved being backstage of course, it has always felt like wonderland. When we were first starting there was always the smell of greasepaint and that's something you never forget even though hardly anyone uses greasepaint these days. If they use any make-up it's pancake applied with a sponge and maybe a little eyeliner. In our early days we used the stick make-up. You'd rub it all over your face, making sure you had no 'mask' by blending it down your neck, then you'd add a little rouge to the cheeks, eyeliner and a spot of red in the corner of each eye. I didn't really know why we did that for some years until someone told me that it was to highlight the eyes and give them a little sparkle under the lights.

You then finish off the whole thing with a powdering to stop the shine. Looking back it now seems like quite a palaver but it was necessary because the limes were so bright. The limes? Those are the big spotlights that beam down from the back of the theatre to light up the performer on stage. They're called limes because in the days before electricity they were powered by a burning lime light.

One thing we have always loved, but especially then, was to walk out on stage before a show or between shows and look out over the footlights at all the seats. Footlights – yes that's virtually another thing of the past. For those that have never seen them they were a row of different coloured lights – red, amber, blue, green and white – that were at your feet between you on the stage and the orchestra pit.

A lot of modern theatres don't have built-in orchestra pits either. We often used to play pantomimes and big variety shows with an orchestra of about sixteen musicians. It was great to have them at pensioner matinees in February as they doubled the audience. Having a drummer was good too because you got all sorts of special effects from him – not always when you expected them!

The poor drummer had the worst job of course as he had to stay in the pit for the entire panto to give us the bangs and crashes, while the violins, trombones and the rest would clear off to the pub until they were needed again. I have to admit that their timing was brilliant because they always managed to get back to their places in the pit in time for the next song without the audience realising they had been missing. Sometimes the MD didn't realise they had been missing either – unless he had been in the pub with them! Don't run away with the idea that musicians drink too much – oh no! They spill most of it!!

Anyway, where was I? Oh yes – standing there on the stage looking at the auditorium. It is something I have always loved. There is something very special about that moment before the people start to come into the theatre to take their seats. The theatre has an atmosphere all of its own when it is empty and a totally different atmosphere when there is an audience. It is not just what you see but what you feel and even what you smell both in the auditorium and backstage.

The smell of the greasepaint and the roar of the crowd are quite unique. You will notice that I have got that the right way round! Talking of smells, did you know that it has always been theatre law that nobody takes cooked food backstage? Even if you were the biggest of stars you had to stick to that law. Fish and chips would be the biggest crime of all.

When we were kids we wondered why and thought it was just a tradition that you didn't do it, but of course we later realised that the smell would linger and find its way onto costumes. It wouldn't be right for a glamorous singing star to look a million dollars as she walked on the stage while the front row were thinking: "That reminds me, what time does the chippy close?"

We also learned when we were kids never to touch anything on stage or in the wings. You don't touch props that belong to a magician, for instance, because you could mess up his entire act. That same rule applies to anyone and everyone. Sometimes you have a prop set exactly where you can get it instantly for a gag. Someone moves it and the gag is ruined and the audience is then distracted wondering what on earth is up with you.

We didn't realise then as kids that we were actually picking up a lot of show business education that was going to hold us in good stead when we started our own careers. Yes, we were raw but we already knew something about theatre etiquette and rules.

We were also picking up the language so when someone mentioned the flies we didn't start looking at our trousers. We knew what front cloths, tabs and front runners were from an early age.

The one thing that frightened the life out of us was when we heard someone say that the ghost would be walking on Friday night. Our hair stood on end and I don't think it has ever gone down since then. Our Dad explained to us that this was an old expression which meant that Friday night was pay night.

One of the great experiences we had in those days was being taken by stage hands up to the grid high above the stage where the cloths hang. Believe me, you had to have a head for heights if you went up there. The walkways are just slats of wood about an inch apart and go from one side of the stage to the other. In some places it is about 100 feet high and looking down makes you feel really sick – at least it did for Barry and me. It is one of those things you should do if you get the chance but you probably won't want to do it again!

These days all the Health and Safety rules have changed a lot of that but don't get me started in that direction because I can get really grumpy about it, or so my wife tells me. I suppose I am in some ways. I just can't stand ridiculous red tape. Sometimes I think you can't say "To Me... To You..." without going on a course and getting a certificate to say you are qualified!

I remember my Dad used to say: "The world's gone mad". I used to think he was crackers but now I feel that he is right but he was about fifty years too early. Now it really has gone mad! He would certainly find it difficult to cope with the things today's comics get away with. He would not believe the language. Remember, he got a two-year ban from BBC radio for a gag that ended "as smooth as a baby's bottom!" A two-year ban for that! He would spin in his grave if he could hear them now.

Anyway, so there we were in Edinburgh at the Palladium for a week and we had a really good week too. We went well in the show, the show itself went well and as far as we were concerned, we only had to wait now for all the work to start rolling in. It did too, but not quite the way we had hoped.

When we got home, it wasn't to a heroes' welcome. Mum made sure our feet were on the ground. "Things have got to change," she said and added that since I had now actually worked for money I would have to start paying National Insurance and all that kind of thing. Then came the real punchline. I would have to go out and get a job! It was no idle threat either. Within a week she had me working at Timpsons Shoe Repairs in Rotherham town centre. I hated every minute of it. It wasn't interesting, it wasn't fun – it wasn't show business!

I stood it for three weeks. I would have lasted longer in the Foreign Legion! Fortunately my brother Colin put a word in for me where he was working, which was T.C. Harrison in

Rotherham. Thanks to Colin I got a job in the body shop doing up second hand cars to go on sale. Barry also worked there in the office so we were together again, probably an error on the part of the management.

We started playing five-a-side football every week at Rawmarsh, another area of Rotherham, and we were doing really well. We played every Wednesday evening and had to catch the half past five bus to get there. The trouble was we didn't clock off work until half past five so it was a mad dash for the bus and hope it was a few minutes late which it usually was.

Someone had a brainwave and a friend of ours at Harrison's who didn't play football agreed to clock off for us which meant that we could leave at a quarter past five and not have to run for the bus.

That worked well until we went in one Thursday morning and came face to face with the manager, the same manager who had needed to see Barry before he went home and had been looking for him after we had left early. Barry's best mate Pete also worked there and he was also in the football team so when the boss couldn't find Barry he started to look for Pete who was also missing.

The upshot was instant dismissal and worse than that was having to go home and explain to Mum. This was the 1960s and finding another job was not that difficult, though. Within a week I'd got another job, this time in Sheffield at a company called Edgar Allen. No they didn't make poes! If you don't understand that one, phone a friend. It was in fact a steel foundry, unusual in Sheffield of course! Well, it is now. That particular company and many like it do not exist any more. When it went they built a shopping complex on the site. It's called Meadowhall. Heard of it?

Anyway, I worked in the office and one of my jobs was to take the time books round to the workers in the factory and then pick them up later so that their wages could be sorted out. I quite enjoyed that because there was a great camaraderie on the shop floor with a lot of laughs. Looking back, I picked up a lot of stuff from those great lads.

To get to work I had to catch a bus from East Herringthorpe to Rotherham and then another bus to Tilsley. Each journey cost me a penny ha'penny, so there and back cost me sixpence a day (5p) or half a crown a week. My Mum gave me my snap every day. Snap? That's what we call a lunch box. I earned £4 a week, kept £1 for myself and gave the rest to my Mum. She paid my bus fares for me out of that so I never overspent and couldn't afford to go to work.

So the pound I had was mine, all mine, and after work I often called at the snooker hall above Burtons Tailors for a game or two. Many jokes have been based on misspent childhood in snooker halls but to me, as a 16-year-old, I enjoyed being there and especially I liked playing on a particular type of machine there. It was like a pinball machine but without the flippers. It had holes numbered 1 to 25 with a bingo card at eye level and the idea of the game was to get three, four or five in a line either vertically, horizontally or from corner to corner. There were various ways you could win as well as the obvious and the prize was a cash payment. The snooker hall wasn't supposed to have a cash paying machine but they did and I really liked it. I was hooked.

I wasn't the only one. There was always a queue at the two machines that played this game. It cost you six pence to have a go and I used to allocate two shillings – enough for four games. I would end then, win or lose. It was rare that I didn't go home with at least £1.10s profit. Sometimes my two shillings would last for ages because I kept winning small amounts and I wouldn't get home until around ten o'clock.

I worked there for about eighteen months and was fairly happy with life although both Barry and I still wished we were working full-time in show business. Still, we were getting by and it seemed that we had found a comfortable way of life. That was fine until one rather special day in February 1965.

Chapter 3

Hi-De-Hi!

Barry was never happy unless he was involved in show business, I suppose that goes for most of us in the family really. Barry bought The Stage newspaper every week and scoured the jobs adverts constantly trying to find something that would be ideal for us. We were not that keen on working the clubs even though we appeared in them regularly. It was better than not working at all but we felt much more at home on a theatre stage.

Still, we were learning the trade all the time and we didn't get tempted to do anything other than a family act – Dad's upbringing about never going 'blue'. He told us that he often had men come up to him in the clubs and ask why he didn't do some dirty jokes. He always used to say: "I can tell you hundreds of blue jokes in the toilets or outside in the car park but there is no way I am going to tell a joke like that in front of women or anyone that might be offended."

Our Dad was never a prude, in fact he was a man's man but he didn't believe in blue comedy in front of women or anyone else that didn't especially want to hear it. He would probably be branded a sexist today because, sadly, it seems that there are a number of women who not only want to hear such jokes but feel they have a right to hear them because they are "as good as any man". Political correctness didn't really exist in Dad's day. I'd better not get on my soapbox, though. Some things are quite right, while other things are just plain ridiculous.

Anyway, one day in February Barry saw an advert in The Stage that was to make a huge change to our lives. It was for a place called Sunshine Holiday Camp in Hayling Island. A strange notion really because the sunshine wasn't guaranteed and Hayling Island isn't an island, it is a promontory. That's a good word, isn't it? Actually Hayling Island is a very nice promontory, a piece of land that juts out into the sea with water all round it except the bit that's joined to the mainland. Anyway, let's say it was nearly an island but not quite and accept that it is called Hayling Island, I don't know why but there it is. That sounds like Harry Worth. That was one of his catchphrases: "My name's Harry Worth, I don't know why, but there it is".

My wife has just told me to get on with it. It is not easy writing your memoirs with your wife looking over your shoulder. I would like to point out to you readers in case you are getting the wrong idea, I wear the trousers in our house. Sue just tells me which pair!

Where was I before she put me off, oh yes, I remember. Barry found us this job and what a brilliant job it was. We had work for six months, including 'digs' which turned out to be a caravan that was at least forty years old and had no running water or heating. It had two bedrooms, a lounge and a sort of kitchen with one low wattage bulb to give us some light.

We didn't care, we were doing our first ever summer season away from home and felt very independent at the age of seventeen. I think that is something every one should try at that age. You have to look after yourself and don't just rely on your Mum and Dad for everything. You grow up pretty quickly. (Actually that last bit isn't really true otherwise Barry and I wouldn't be the Chuckle Brothers).

So, there we were looking after ourselves. We had money in our pockets as we were getting £12 a week between us and our food was supplied along with our accommodation.

That accommodation might only have been an antique caravan but we had a lot of fun in there, I can tell you!

Hang on a minute, wife's looking over shoulder again.

It was tiring work as we were busy near enough all day, not just at show time. We had to be on duty at 7.25am in the dining hall to welcome the campers in for breakfast. Have you ever tried encouraging someone with a hangover to eat eggs, bacon and beans first thing in the morning?!

Next on our agenda was a daily pep talk from the entertainments manager and then we were off to the sports shop, which had to be open for 8.30am. Barry and I had the job of handing out the table tennis bats, snooker equipment, roller skates, cricket bats, putting clubs and balls, bowls, footballs, the lot. We handed over what they wanted and they handed us their key. I don't ever remember anyone making a run for it with a ping-pong ball so the system must have worked okay. I must say we looked pretty smart. We had to wear white shoes and trousers, a white shirt and a bright yellow jumper. Barry looked like an anaemic daffodil.

We had the amusement arcade where we worked as well and I soon learned the knack of getting free games from my pal Ken who was in charge of the arcade and had all the keys to the machines. I was mad on pinball machines and would play for hours, given the chance. There was never any question of winning prizes or cash, it was just getting free games. On hot sunny days and Saturday mornings it was usually quiet in the arcade so if there was nobody around Ken would open up the machine for me and I would be glued to it until Barry pulled me away.

So, what a job we had. It was a perfect job for meeting young ladies, except that they seemed to perform this strange ritual. They would hang about near you in twos or threes and keep giving you glances. Then when they knew they had your attention they would turn away from you and leave you wondering what it was all about. It's a bit like lads giving a girl a wolf whistle. Why do they do that? I've never yet seen a girl attracted to someone who gave her a wolf whistle and go up to him and say "Okay, where and what time?" It's strange the things we do for no real reason.

So there we were in the sports shop for six days a week but we also did what we were really booked for – we entertained in the evenings. Barry and I loved every minute of it. The shows were all themed, like we might do The Sound of Music. It wasn't the show of the name but we would do songs from that musical and others too. Each entertainer sang a couple of songs or played an instrumental.

Barry and I mostly did the comedy and it went well every time because the audience knew us from what we were doing during the day so it was like them having their pals up there on the stage and they gave us a lot of support, laughing at almost anything we did. It was a great grounding for us and any other act. We also did some song and dance routines in those days, although Dad always told us not to be too versatile. "If you do all sorts in your act, the promoters will just use you to fill the bill instead of building you up as a main act," he told us. It was good advice.

We realised that he was right and eventually we dropped the song and dance and concentrated totally on the comedy. It was quite a risk and not the easiest thing when playing a working men's club in Sunderland! If they didn't like your comedy, you had no escape route.

Anyway, this first season as a double act was a great education. After the stage show we had to go to the ballroom and dance with lady campers. We were under strict instructions that we were not to dance with anyone under the age of forty. We were stunned by that – all those young ladies and we were not allowed to dance with them! Mind you, at midnight the evening always finished with us entertainers singing *Good night campers* to the tune of *Good night sweetheart*, then it was every man for himself.

Wife's back.

Often we would all go to the El Sombrero café for a late night cuppa and to unwind a bit. Drinking alcohol wasn't as big as it is today and most young people congregated at cafés. Just to prove that we were real intellectuals, one of our pastimes was to get the silver paper from an empty cigarette packet and carefully part the silver from the paper bit. You would then chew on the paper whole moulding the silver bit into something like the FA Cup. Once it was well chewed you would put the paper into the cup bit and launch it towards the ceiling. If you did it right it would stick firmly to the ceiling. By the end of the season there were hundreds of these stuck to the ceiling and it started looking like a cave. We thought it was very artistic. Others had different views of course.

There was some great music around during that season too. We had hit after hit from The Beatles, The Stones, The Byrds and my personal favourites, The Kinks. The jukebox was never given a minute's rest and the favourite plays of the season were

Help by The Beatles and *I Got You Babe* from Sonny and Cher. Great songs which always evoke memories when I hear them.

The season was great, hard work but great and we were a little sad when it came to an end. One thing was definite, we were now professional entertainers and we could not go back to having "proper jobs". We went back to Rotherham and lived off a little dole money – about £3 a week – and some occasional working men's clubs. We tried everything to get a panto season but we were always told the same thing: "Tell us where you are doing panto and we'll come and see you with a view to something for next year." To get a panto we had to already have a panto – a vicious circle.

We were broke most of the time but we survived as a double act and looked forward to hopefully getting another summer season somewhere. We did an audition for a revue company and were optimistic that we got the job. We did but it turned out the revue was only part of the job. We had passed our audition to become Butlins Redcoats at Cliftonville, Margate, on the Kent coast.

Once again we were to gain some great memories, starting with the Saturday train journey. We arrived in London at St. Pancras, got the Underground to Waterloo and then the train to Margate before getting a bus to Cliftonville. It seemed a long haul in those days and we were relieved when we got off the bus and were met by the entertainments manager who gave us a warm handshake and a big smile and told us that he had heard great things about us. We were tired but quite pleased to hear that – until he told us that we wanted us to start that evening at the Norfolk Hotel at about eight o'clock.

We were taken aback because we were a bit shattered and just wanted to get some sleep. We were a bit surprised to be asked to do a gig in a hotel but of course, Butlins Cliftonville was not like the big holiday camps, it was a series of hotels, slightly more upmarket actually.

Anyway, there we were having arrived at about six o'clock and with two hours to get ourselves in a fit state to go and entertain unexpectedly. The nerves kicked in straight away although we didn't quite go as far as panic. There was no need for us to worry though. The audience was probably the best we had ever had up to that point and laughed at everything. We did a twenty minute spot and got a standing ovation at the end of it. We thought we were dreaming but we were the toast of Cliftonville after that.

The word got out and we found ourselves in demand to do a spot in the touring revue show every Sunday and occasionally went to the Butlins Hotel in Brighton to do a spot. They even sent us to Ramsgate for a week, which was quite a compliment. Butlins was brilliant for us and it was a very special year in 1966.

We all know what happened in 1966 of course. England versus Germany. That had happened twice before – in 1914 and 1939 – with Germany kicking off each time and England winning! I just pinched that from Alan Randall who was a great pal of ours and used to say that in his act after England won the World Cup in that year: "3-0 to us", he used to day. It was not politically correct and not a joke you would make today, but funny at that time. It just goes to show how things change. Alan was a fantastic George Formby impersonator, though, and one of the world's greatest vibraphone players, a tremendously talented entertainer who, sadly, is no longer with us.

I actually missed the World Cup Final. Although we were storming as entertainers we still had to fulfil our duties as Redcoats. One of my jobs was projectionist. The daytime shows were cartoons in the children's cinema. We showed *Bugs Bunny*,

Road Runner, Mr Magoo, Tom and Jerry and loads of others. By the time October came round I knew every word of every cartoon. Two afternoons a week we showed real films and that season it was *The Ipcress File* on Tuesdays and a Richard Widmark war film, *The Bedford Incident,* with Sidney Poitier on one of the other days. Great film by the way.

I very nearly drowned during that season, too. I was with another Redcoat who was also the lifeguard and we were chatting up a couple of nurses by the pool. One of them said they had never seen me in the pool and I told them I couldn't swim. That was true. I can now but I couldn't then. They didn't believe me and tried to get me into the water, fully clothed. One pulled and one pushed and in the end I fell in.

I remember going under the water and thinking that my pal would jump in and save me. My feet didn't touch the bottom and my head was below the water level. I held my breath and started thrashing about. I didn't start to splutter but I felt as if I wasn't breathing and everything seemed to start going black. Then I felt someone enter the water beside me and push me upwards. The next thing I remember was being held by my waist, head down between my knees and water pouring out of my mouth and nose.

My mate was very apologetic. He thought I had been joking about not being able swim and it was only when I stopped thrashing about that he realised something was seriously wrong. I was grateful that he did something at all otherwise there might have been just one Chuckle Brother by now. At least I got a free brandy and the rest of the day off but I also got into a bit of trouble because I wouldn't say who had done it.

Butlins meant long days of course, starting at 7am with the Tannoy system playing *A Summer's Day* and a loud Bing Bong sound followed by a happy voice saying "Good Morning

Guests!" You never called them campers at an upmarket Butlins Hotel. Once again we started at 7.25am and sat at each table of eight for breakfast. That was where the day's entertainment began, whether the guests were ready for it or not.

I had a couple of hours off then until the cartoons started at half past ten. Quite often I played them to myself but they had to be shown otherwise someone would complain that they were not available as advertised. One evening a week we had filmed horse racing. That was really my favourite night of the week. There were eight races and you could bet two shillings on any horse numbers from 1 to 8. Even if there were more horses running, the winners would be numbered 1 to 8. I was the projectionist of course. Each film was sealed until just before the race. Once I had broken the seal I wired it up and ran the first sequence. A code number appeared before the race then I'd pause the film until the betting stopped.

After four or five weeks I realised that the same films were coming back every now and then so I started to memorise the numbers of films in which the No 4 horse won. I would get one of the guests to back it for me and with that I made a few quid extra during the season. I never went mad otherwise I would have been found out. You don't kill the fatted calf.

We earned £25 a week that season and at the end of it we also received a £65 bonus to take home with us. Both Barry and I had taken some driving lessons in Margate during that summer and the week before we went home to Rotherham we both took our tests. We both failed and put it down to not knowing the Margate streets well enough.

Within a few weeks of returning to Rotherham I took mine again after one lesson and this time I passed. Barry tried and failed but it was all because of one silly mistake. I taught him how to put that right and he then passed pretty quickly.

When we came out of the test centre with Barry also now a fully-fledged driver we bought a local newspaper and started looking at the cars for sale. One jumped out at us straight away. It was a black Ford 500cwt Thames van born in 1957 and having had one careful owner. That's the one for us, we thought and decided to go to the farm in Wickersley near Rotherham where the van was kept. We phoned the farmer first and he gave us directions from the bus stop.

That bus journey was pretty exciting. We were going to get our first transport! We followed the farmer's directions and soon were trudging up a farm track until we finally arrived in this typical farmyard. Sure enough there was a black van with no back doors, flat tyres and chickens jumping in and out of it. Barry could not hide his disappointment and said out loud: "You must be joking!"

The farmer arrived at just that moment and couldn't stop laughing, which didn't help Barry's mood until the farmer pointed out that the van was not that one but another one round the back of the yard. We followed him and sure enough there was a really nice looking van, clean and in good condition. We eagerly paid him the £25 asking price and he disappeared into the house for a while before returning with our "change" that we were not expecting. He gave us four half-crowns (10s or 50p if you prefer) and said it was an old farming thing that you always give change when you sell something. It was for good luck and we certainly thought that we had been lucky to get such a van and some change as well.

That Ford Thames van was great. It even had air conditioning, although when it rained your feet and trousers got wet because there were massive holes at your feet and it felt like you were driving a sieve. We kept putting cardboard down but of course that soon got wet and turned into papier maché.

The van also had just one wiper and once on a journey to a gig the blade flew off, so we stopped and wrapped a handkerchief round the wiper and carried on. That didn't last long as the wiper objected and stopped working. Then we had another brainwave and tied some string round the blade and handkerchief, then as I drove Barry kept on pulling the string so that we could see where we were going. It would have been so much easier if it had simply stopped raining! Youngsters today don't have half the fun we had, do they? Do they?!

The van had no windscreen washer, they were extras in those days. There was no heater or radio either but then there were no motorways and there was nothing like the traffic we have now. Most people couldn't afford to run a car. We had to because of our work and I was the only one of my mates who had even a half ownership of a vehicle. The van did have a double seat fitted in the back even though there were no windows. That was handy for taking a girl home and….

Hello love, are you back again???

I would often be the chauffeur for the lads and we would go to the Grapes at Dalton and then on to the Penny Farthing at Doncaster. There was usually Phil Cliff, Mick Churm and myself and we had some great nights out. We were into Motown and soul music and I was always a big fan of the Supremes, still am.

The van was part of the team and I remember at the end of 1966 when we had a Christmas Eve booking at a working men's club somewhere in Barnsley. It took us forever to find the place and when we got there we had been double booked and were not to take part. It was a good job really because we didn't get there until about ten o'clock at night.

The van was very low on petrol but we guessed we could make it home. We were trying to keep whatever cash we had to last us another week. How wrong we were.

I coaxed the van, freewheeled wherever I could and got to the Kimberworth area, about a mile and a half outside Rotherham, when finally the van spluttered to a halt. It was a freezing cold Christmas Eve, about 10.45pm and not a soul about. We kicked ourselves for being so stupid as to not put a gallon of fuel in when we had the chance. It was only about 4s 9d in those days at the Globe petrol station near where we lived (about 24p in today's money).

We decided that if we could just push the van to the top of the hill we could freewheel into Rotherham, so that's what we did. Barry and I pushed the van all the way to the top. Well, one of us did! It took us about three quarters of an hour to push the van about three hundred yards to the top of the hill and then we jumped in and off we went. It was then I realised that I had got the wrong hill and that there was another one before we actually got into Rotherham. We freewheeled down and up the next hill as far as we could until the van stopped again. We tried to push it again but we were absolutely shattered.

Then a miracle happened. A car came in the opposite direction and stopped to see what the problem was. There were two young guys and we thought they might have helped push us to the top of the hill, but it was better than that. The driver told Barry to jump in and he took him to get a gallon of petrol. He was a great Rotherham guy and helped us to get home. We thanked him of course and wished him all the best for Christmas but we never got his name and have never seen him again to this day. If he is reading this, get in touch so that we can say a proper thanks.

We finally got home at about one in the morning. Christmas Eve 1966 had been quite an experience – it had also been Barry's birthday!

The van, with all its foibles, served us well until one day

we went to Manchester to appear at a club and going over the Woodhead Pass we bumped over a small hole in the road. We heard a loud bang and stopped to look at the damage. We couldn't actually see any so we drove on but kept hearing a kind of bumping and thumping sound. We tried to ignore it and decided that it was probably nothing really and that our brother Colin would fix it for us the next day. He was a great brother and is sadly missed. He always looked after our cars and those of our brothers Jimmy and Brian.

We took the van to him the next day and he told us it was almost a miracle that we were still driving it. The chassis had totally snapped in two and Barry and I could have gone our separate ways at any time. There was only one place for the van – the scrap yard. We took it to the yard and it was like taking a pet to the vet's for a one-way journey. We waved it goodbye and accepted a £5 note from the scrap dealer, robbery really as we had just spent £12 on a brand new battery.

We then saw a Ford Prefect for sale in a garage. It was a 'sit up and beg' type with fenders and had been brand new in 1953. They only wanted £13 for it. I know that sounds ridiculous now but there was no warranty with it. What you saw was really what you paid for. We had a gig at Cleethorpes coming up and had to have some transport so we bought it. I actually thought it was a lovely old car and it got us where we needed to go – for exactly three weeks to the day before a horrible banging noise from the engine told everyone that the big ends had gone. So, another trip to the scrap yard and this time we were given just £3, but at least the battery was a rubbish one.

We still needed wheels though and then we saw a beautiful square-shaped Ford Popular. It looked clean and modern, had a heater that worked and even a radio. It was £125 which was a lot of money. However, we had bought cheaply before and that had not worked so we decided that we should take our first steps into the world of hire purchase and bought it.

So, now we took stock and we suddenly realised that we were professional entertainers and could afford an "expensive car" costing £125. We had made it! No, not really, still a long way to go.

Chapter 4

Icy Encounters of the Scary Kind

If we were under any illusion that we were anywhere near stardom it didn't last long. We were delighted to be getting work and having wheels but we knew really that there was still a long way to go. We were young and didn't really have any great dreams of stardom. We were mostly just pleased that we didn't have to have a "proper job".

Having said that, it was by now 1967 and things were definitely getting better for Barry and me. We put ourselves up for an audition at a night club in Nottingham which we thought might help us get a bigger audience as the audition was for the massively popular TV show *Opportunity Knocks* which was presented by Hughie Green.

The club was packed with hopefuls and Hughie Green was also there in person to watch the acts. The various turns were not filmed at this stage, it was just a question of doing your

49

bit and then leaving or staying at the back to watch everyone else. We were told that they would not tell us there and then if we had made it but they would get in touch eventually if they wanted us. Television is often like that. They ask if you can do something, decide that you can and then you don't hear any more. Just when you have almost forgotten about it you suddenly get a phone call asking if you are busy tomorrow.

Anyway, it came to our turn so Barry and I went on and did our routine which we had to force into a three minute spot. We went down a storm, the place exploded into laughter and cheers and Hughie Green stood up and asked us to do some of it again so that they could film it and take it back to the studio. We were in! So much for having to wait until they got in touch.

We were thrilled of course and couldn't wait to tell everybody. We did the show in February from the ATV studios in Manchester. That was our very first television appearance and it felt great. We wanted more of the same but it took some time coming. Still, that *Opportunity Knocks* appearance did help us a lot. We were already booked for a summer season but on the strength of our TV slot we were offered our first pantomime season, playing in *Babes in the Wood* in Malvern.

Our summer season was in *The Minstrel Show* at the Savoy, Southsea. That sounds a bit posh doesn't it, but in fact it was an upstairs ballroom opposite the pier. Still, we enjoyed it and it was good to know that we were already booked for a winter season too and that we would not have to be scratching around trying to find something to do when the summer ended.

If you ever start to believe your own publicity in this business you can guarantee that something will bring you down to earth with a big bang. For us it was usually our cars. The *Babes in the Wood* panto was a great experience. After the show on New Year's Eve the whole company was invited to a party over the nearby mountain range at a night club where one of the panto artistes was also appearing.

On the way we hit a patch of ice like a sheet of glass but it was okay as we were not going very fast up the side of the mountain. We had a good time and came out at about two in the morning to find that it was snowing quite hard. We were a bit worried that it might quickly become too deep for us to drive through and get home but we took our chances anyway. It all went well going back up the hill but as we came down the other side I remembered the ice patch on a sharp bend. I tried to take the bend gently, using the handbrake to help slow us down without going into a spin but the car had thoughts of its own and tried to get its rear end to overtake us on the right and then on the left as I spun the wheel to try and keep it straight.

The snow was now whipping down so hard that we couldn't see a thing and we thought that at any moment we were going to drop over the edge and start flying through the air. What would have happened does not bear thinking about, but what actually happened was that the car suddenly straightened and began behaving normally. I hope that it doesn't sound wrong to say that God must have looked after us that night. Perhaps He knew we were going to turn into the Chuckle Brothers. Whatever the reason, a big thanks from us!

The panto ran for two weeks in Malvern and then the whole show moved to Bridlington for another week. We gave two of the dancers a lift in our car – for no reason other than being a couple of nice guys! As it happened they proved to be useful because we had only been driving for an hour when our fan belt went. One pair of tights was produced (not ours, theirs!) and off we went again.

That was not the only trouble there as we found that the car's alternator was knackered and the lights on the car got dimmer and dimmer as the engine also began to splutter. Somehow we managed to limp home to Rotherham and our Colin came to the rescue once again. He was still working at T.C. Harrison which was a Ford main dealers and since our car was a Ford, Col could get his hands on a replacement alternator and fit it pretty quickly. Col worked for the company for 49 years if you include his two years of National Service which he served in the RAF (5044362 Elliott C.D.). I remember his number because Mum used to write to him all the time when he was in Northern Ireland.

Colin came to our rescue many, many times over the years. Once our Cortina came to a sudden halt in Norfolk, just south of King's Lynn. The engine would not budge and we had no AA cover. We phoned Colin and he told us exactly what the problem was without even seeing it. With that he jumped in his car and drove all the way to us in Norfolk from Rotherham. He spent two and a half hours driving to us and two and a half hours driving back again. The actual job of replacing the distributor took him ten minutes.

That was so typical of our Col who helped us and many other people countless times. There wasn't much we could do in return because neither Barry nor I had that sort of skill but we did knock out a bungalow wall for him. Before you ask, yes he did want it knocking out and no, I didn't drive into it. Barry and I took it down brick by brick. It took us ages but nothing like the effort that Col always made to help us.

As I said, cars bring you back down to earth if you start to think you are better than you are.

After that great panto season at Malvern and Bridlington we went on tour with Ronnie Cryer in the same minstrel show we had been doing the previous summer. This was not in theatres though, we did a tour of working men's clubs and we found that it was much better if we were part of a package. We actually started to enjoy them.

Once when we were driving to a club in South Wales one of the girls in the show was travelling with us and suddenly realised that she had left a costume behind at the flat we were all renting in Penarth. I turned the car round – a Zodiac – and started to drive back. We went round a bend and had to go up a hill. A big van was coming down the hill and there was not enough passing room so I stopped the car and went into reverse.

To our horror the van just kept coming and smashed right into the front of us, damaging our front offside wing. We were tight up against a wall so I had to climb out of a window to speak to the driver. To our amazement he then started to reverse with us hooked on his van. He must have dragged us twenty feet with me half in and half out of the window before he stopped. I showed him my documents but he refused to show his. In the end I took his registration number and sent one of the girls to phone the police. They soon arrived and took statements from everyone. To be honest they could not have been more helpful.

It all went even more sour though when we had to go back to Penarth to the court a month later. The police assured me that it was normal routine but in the end I came out of there minus £60 and with three points on my licence. The police seemed as shocked as I was, especially since the lad got off scot-free and had the nerve to grin and hoot at me when he drove off afterwards.

Was it because I was a Northerner and he was a local lad? Was he related to the magistrate? Who knows, but I told the police that if I was ever in their town again and saw someone robbing a bank I would look the other way. They were very understanding, to their credit.

Once again Colin came to our rescue with the car. He could not believe that we had managed to get all the way to Rotherham because quite a bit of damage had been done to the engine as well as the body of the car. It was not so much "To Me... To You..." as "From us to him broken and from him to us repaired!"

That *Opportunity Knocks* appearance was also seen by Jack Billing, an impressario who booked us for the 1968 summer season in Rhyl – and what a show he put on. It was a stage ice show called *Minstrels on Ice* at the Coliseum Theatre which he also owned at that time. I don't think the likes of this show had been seen before, certainly not in Rhyl in 1968 because it combined the very popular production of a minstrel show with an ice rink on the stage.

From the first day to the last of that twelve-week season the audience queued in a huge snake up and down the promenade. We did two shows a night for six nights a week and every one of them was sold out.

Of course having an ice rink on stage did present some unusual problems. Keeping the ice frozen was the hardest job. This was not synthetic ice but the real thing. The refrigeration unit had a cut-out switch to stop it from over-heating because of constant use. That meant that now and then it had to be physically switched on again. Since the theatre was empty overnight there was nobody to switch it on and in hot weather the ice could start to melt.

This happened once when the season was about three weeks old. We had to do the show with about an inch of water on the ice. Let me tell you that Barry and I did not skate, that was left to the professional skaters who performed various routines, really good too. No, Barry and I worked on what they call "treads" which were in front of the ice close to the audience or behind the ice with skaters performing in front of us.

Our first summer season at Sunshine Holiday Camp,
Hayling Island in 1965.

First double act picture of the Chuckle Brothers. Paul aged 3 and Barry aged 6.

Paul school photograph. As you look at the picture Paul is front row and far right. Cute!!

Barry aged 11.

Paul aged 7.
Just look at those
ears!!!

Our beautiful mum.

Our beloved dad in 1982 a few months before he passed away.

Us with our beautiful and still missed mum in
Rhyl, North Wales, 1958.

Paul, Barry and
Uncle Bob on
Ramsgate beach.

Paul on Ramsgate beach aged 12. Barry was
in his first summer season there.

Barry with cousin Elsena, both looking a bit sea sick.

Paul trying out early ChuckleVision faces.

Our dad, second from the right, with Peter Sellers waving his hat in Burma during World War II.

A publicity photo of our father Gene Patton from around the 1920s.

A GREAT REVUE COMEDIAN
GENE PATTON

Paul, Barry and cousin Elsena on platform awaiting our train. Steam trains in those days.

Brother Jimmy's wedding in 1964 at Hailsworth in Suffolk. From left to right: Paul, Barry, Auntie Ethel, cousins Alan, Jim and Val. The two on the end we're not too sure of.

A publicity photo of Barry when he worked as a solo comedian in 1961.

Barry publicity picture 1960.

Paul aged 15 and Barry aged 18. Before Paul grew from 4' 10" to 5' 11" in two years.

Hiding from Barry (been a habit for many, many years).

*From 1963.
Hard to believe
Barry was taller
than me.*

*Paul in Margate
season (Butlins)
on way out for the
night.*

*Paul (above) and
Barry as The
Harman Brothers.*

Here we are as the Harman Brothers in 1965 for our first summer season at Sunshine Holiday Camp, Hayling Island.

Speaks for itself. We were trying to make it look like it was our car!

Paul & Barry late 1970s.

Sand Dance performed at Cliffs Pavilion, Southend, 1980.

A young Paul snapped whilst out trying his hand at photography.

Charity football match in 1981. Far right on the front row is a very young Bobby Davro and above him Jimmy Cricket. Dig those curly perms on Paul & Barry.

We did set foot on the ice of course and in the opening scene Barry, myself and another guy called Malcolm would walk across the ice to the beat of introduction music and then onto the treads where we performed. I led the way and Barry brought up the rear and on this one occasion as we walked across the ice in time to the music I suddenly heard a splash behind me and a huge laugh from the audience. I looked round in time to see Barry flat on his back with his legs in the air and completely soaked. Without a twitch, Barry stood up, turned around and walked back off the stage, still to the beat of the music. Malcolm and I couldn't sing for laughing.

A strange thing happened to me during that summer season, something that sends the shivers down my spine even when I think about it now. I had my first ghostly encounter! Oh yes I did!

We had rented a one bedroom flat for the summer. Barry being the older one got first choice and chose to have the bedroom, which meant that I had a put-up bed in the corner of the lounge. It was quite a big lounge really and I put the bed just under the window. On this particular night it was really hot. We had only just got to bed and I was lying there thinking about how very hot it was. I turned over to face the wall and pushed the sheet down to my waist. Suddenly I got very cold and pulled the sheet back up and around my neck. "What's going on?" I wondered. One minute I am really hot and the next minute freezing cold. I didn't feel ill. This was something else.

Then I suddenly got this horrible feeling that someone was standing behind me. My eyes were wide open and staring at the wallpaper. I didn't dare move. I just waited to see what was going to happen next. There was not a sound but I felt the sheet moving down and the feeling that someone was getting into bed with me. Suddenly the coldness went and the room became really warm again. The feeling that someone was there just went away and everything seemed normal again.

I plucked up the courage to move and look around and nothing seemed to have moved or changed in any way. It's funny how you notice things and I started to stare at the wall at the foot end of the bed. There were two alcoves and I started to imagine that there had been a body bricked up in there or something like that.

Nothing else happened and when the landlord came for his rent I told him of my experience the night before. He laughed and told me that the building we were in used to be a brothel in the 1920s. (For the kids – a brothel is a place where you can get a bowl of broth). It made me wonder what exactly had got into bed with me! It never happened again. An acquaintance once told me that most people get the chance once or twice to be in the presence of a ghost and if you have the courage to look it straight in the eye that spirit would look after you for the rest of your life.

Now, supposing he was right. Supposing I had looked and it had been a nice looking young lady who would then take care of me for the rest of my life. She would never get any older even if I did. Maybe I should have looked? Mind you, knowing my luck, if I had done it would probably have been a huge, hairy sailor, six feet six inches in all directions and none too partial! No, I did the right thing. What would you have done?

Changing the subject, Freddie Starr was just along the seafront from our show with his group The Delmonts. He had been on *Opportunity Knocks* for several weeks earlier that year and was pulling in good audiences. For those who don't know or remember, *Opportunity Knocks* worked by audiences' and viewers' votes. If you won you came back the next week. We did two weeks on the show but Freddie did about six weeks which showed that people really liked him and it was no surprise that they all wanted to see him during that season at Rhyl.

You might remember that Barry and Freddie had been in the Singing Scholars together so they were already mates from back in 1960. Fred was sharing a house with his band and one night they had a huge row. Freddie came round to our flat for a couple of days while peace was restored.

He used to really chill out with us and slept on our settee. It was funny because he was a quiet, ordinary sort of bloke, didn't snore and you hardly knew he was there unless someone knocked on the door. It was as if someone had just switched on the stage lights because he immediately became the performer and stayed that way until the person left, when he would switch off and became quiet and relaxed again. What a star!

When we were at Malvern in pantomime a man called John Hilvers came to see us at a matinee performance. He was a theatre director and during the panto season they go from theatre to theatre to see the shows and the artistes appearing in them. A tip from our Dad did us proud and we always pass it on to young performers – no matter what time the performance or how many are in the audience, give it your best shot. If there are only thirty people sitting in the theatre they will have paid as much as those people who are sitting in a packed auditorium so they deserve to see at least as good a show as anyone else. It is easy to go through the motions but being a performer means exactly that – work hard for the great people who have paid to see you no matter how many of them there are.

Well, we were giving it our best in this matinee when John was in the audience. We didn't know it at the time of course. John loved what he saw and booked us for his panto the following year at Swansea. That was for the 1968-69 panto season and we were there for three months, which was a brilliantly long season.

It was a brilliant show too with Wayne Fontana topping the bill, an orchestra of twelve musicians and sixteen girl dancers. It was *Jack and the Beanstalk* and Barry and I were the henchmen as well as playing the panto cow. Barry was the front end of the cow and I was the udder part. The cow was called Jessy by the way and we both felt a right "Jessie" playing it.

Barry couldn't see very much through the cow's mouth and I couldn't see anything other than the floor and Barry's rear end, which is not the best view in town. There was a yellow strip on the stage which marked the cow's exit to avoid banging into scenery. One night Barry saw the yellow strip and headed for it. Unfortunately it was another yellow strip and we ended up piling through the door of the Dame's house. Barry tripped up and I tripped over him. From the front of the auditorium all they could see was a heap of cow with two lots of cow legs sticking out through the door. The audience was in hysterics, especially as we struggled and failed to get up until a stage hand dragged us through the back and shut the door – that just added to the fun.

The funniest things that happen are usually not rehearsed which is why the outtakes of *ChuckleVision* have proved to be so popular.

Another thing I remember about that panto was seeing a young Keith Harris sat in the audience. Orville wasn't with him of course, I think he was just an egg at that stage. Keith's uncle was the drummer and Keith was totally in love with stage comedy. I think he still is, but for some time now he has been providing the laughs himself.

Anyway, that was a great panto and since then we have played pantomime just about every year and we hope to be doing so for many more years yet. Pantos are just great fun. As well as being the henchmen in *Jack and the Beanstalk* we have been captain and mate in *Dick Whittington*, and Chinese policemen in *Aladdin*.

We often used old routines which were also well used by the great Laurel and Hardy. I don't like using the word genius but those two were real comic geniuses, or genii or whatever you want to call them. They were more brilliant than brilliant. If you get a chance to look at any of their old movies, do it and watch out for all the little things you may not have noticed before. They never missed an opportunity for a gag.

For instance they might come in through a door and without you noticing, the doorknob would come off in Stan's hand. He would look at it puzzled, shrug and then put it back. That was the end of the gag – or was it? Every time they went through a door, the same thing would happen, never when Ollie touched it but always when Stan did. Running gags like that were a big part of their fantastic comedy and they had hundreds of them in every film.

We tried to include things like that too with our *ChuckleVision* shows and also now our stage shows. The beauty of television is that you can put some little gags in that some people will notice and laugh while others will not. It is entirely up to the audience at home. When we get a script we look at it of course and work out what we are going to do, but it is really only when we are on location and running through the script properly that the visual gags come to life. Much depends on the set but sometimes we spot something that might work and the reaction from the crew will tell us that it is a good one, so keep it in.

Anyway, back to Swansea and after pantomime we went straight back to the social clubs. When I say straight back, I mean just that. We worked on the last night of the panto. We did a final matinee performance and then packed everything before the final evening performance. Immediately after the show we jumped in the car and drove home through the night for a couple of hours sleep before getting off early in the morning to appear at noon in West Hartlepool, the start of a two week club tour of Sunderland and the area nearby.

We were a bit drained when we left Swansea. It was not easy because when you say goodbye to everyone you have been working with for three months it is quite an emotional experience. You want it to go on forever. It probably sounds silly but that's show business and show people for you. There's a good chance we shall work together again but at that time of saying goodbye it is as if you are going off to Australia and will never see anyone you know ever again.

I told you it was silly.

We didn't mind going to the Sunderland area because the people there are always a brilliant audience at the Empire Theatre. They are not quite the same at the social clubs though and we were totally shattered when we arrived at the Boiler Makers Club. They put us on stage at half past twelve and wanted two spots from us.

So there we were, yesterday being loved by big audiences at a marvellous theatre in panto in Swansea and today the lunchtime challenge of trying to please people in a working men's club in the North who almost despised you before you set foot on the stage. I don't know why they booked us really because it was just for a couple of hundred working men who were having a pint while the wife was at home cooking the Sunday roast. Anyway, after our first spot they said they didn't want us any more and paid us half our fee.

Fortunately that evening we were in another club in Sunderland and they were totally different. The concert chairman came into the dressing room after our first spot with a big grin on his face and told us how brilliant we were. Then he added: "The Boiler Makers Club secretary phoned me earlier and told me you were crap. I told him I like to make up my own mind. He must be mad to think that. Well done lads."

That is so typical of life in the working men's clubs. You never knew if you would have a good night or a bad one. Another example was at another Sunderland club where we worked at lunchtime. Our opening gag was greeted with a great roar of laughter that went on and on. We thought they must have been taking the mick because it was at least two minutes before we could do our next gag. When we finally did our next gag it was greeted by silence. One minute the six hundred men in there laughed their heads off and the next minute it was like a doctor's waiting room.

We got on with our routine and the silence was only broken by a few of the men starting to chat among themselves. We finished the spot rather quickly and took a break, with just a little applause as we went off. We started to change out of our stage clothes but when the concert secretary came in he wondered why we were preparing to go home.

"They hated us," said Barry.

"What do you mean?" asked the concert secretary. "The place is still full. If they didn't like you they would have gone to the other club up the road."

So, we went back for our second spot but after a couple of minutes they started to leave and go home for their dinner. The secretary was happy though and wanted to book us back again. We just looked at each other and turned down the offer.

Yes, the working men's clubs were like playing Russian roulette. You could get a brilliant audience at one club and then play another club across the road and really suffer at the hands of an audience who hated you just because you'd turned up.

After we won *New Faces* in 1974 we made it a policy that we would never do those clubs again. It reached the point where you had to be at least blue, if not filthy, and that was not what we did. We were also keen to get into television and we didn't want that kind of reputation as that would, in those days, have also meant that TV wouldn't touch us. That has changed of course, but we still wouldn't do blue material.

The summer season we had done at Rhyl led to us getting booked into Prestatyn Holiday Camp for the next summer. We were booked for two shows a week, one on a Sunday evening and the other on the Friday, the campers' last night of the week. We were top of the bill on both shows and could near enough do what we liked. The show opened with a big production and ended with a finale which involved everyone on the show but our main spot was just Barry and me doing a load of gags, sketches and songs. It was hard work but good fun and we went well all season.

Barry actually met his first wife there. He calls her his first wife just to keep her on her toes. They have been married for more than forty years so he hasn't decided to trade her in yet. Anne was doing summer season at the Derbyshire Miners in Rhyl in a double act with a pal. They were dancers and did different routines. We went there on a night out with some mates, ended up dancing with the two girls and that was it. Little did we know that the following spring we would appear on the same bill as them at the City Varieties Theatre in Leeds and that romance would blossom for Barry and Anne.

You might think that we had had enough of Sunderland but we always liked the place and when we were offered pantomime there for the 1969-1970 season it seemed like a good place to see the old year out and the new year in. It was *Jack and the Beanstalk* again, this time with Derek Dene as top of the bill and us as the henchmen and the cow again. Derek was great and we had a lot of laughs between us. Because he was a good pro you could throw in lots of extra gags.

Derek had a special gag for the cow. You always try to have a milking scene involving the cow. Jack would get the job of milking the reluctant cow. He would put the bucket down while he fetched the stool and of course, the cow would kick the bucket away. Then he'd get the bucket back and find that the stool had been kicked away. That went on for a while until he finally sat down and went for the udders which I then pulled up into the cow out of the way. This happened a couple of times then Derek would say that he'd warm his hands. He held them over the footlights and then when he came back the udders would fall off as if by accident. The audience then saw my hand appear from under the cow and grab them back.

It started off as a three minute routine but by the time we had added bits it lasted about seven minutes but always got lots of laughs. For a couple of shows Barry and I swapped places because my back was killing me. Derek said it was amazing how different it made the whole cow. We did the same things but it was different. You wouldn't think that would happen but it did. Derek died a few years ago and is still sadly missed. He was a great guy.

Sunderland was also the place where I was late on stage one day. I have to admit that I was paying some attention to the wardrobe girl and lost track of the time. I was sent into a panic when I heard our intro music playing. Our room was on the top floor and I almost jumped down all the stairs to get to the stage level. As I got to the stage I could see Barry doing funny walks all over the set, with the band in hysterics. Barry wasn't too pleased though and let me know afterwards.

I confess that throughout the years if anyone was going to miss our entrance it would usually be me, I used to get distracted easily. The number of times that has happened to Barry you could count on one hand with fingers to spare.

The panto went well again and we were offered by Terry "Toby Jug" Cantor the following year's panto at the City Varieties Theatre in Leeds. That was the theatre used for the fantastic *The Good Old Days* TV show but while we loved the theatre we didn't fancy the panto. The theatre is quite small and after Swansea and Sunderland it felt that we were going backwards. Terry had an ace card though. If we did the panto he could offer us Olde Time Music Hall in Leeds for the spring, followed by fourteen weeks in Skegness and then back to Leeds for another four weeks. The panto would run from December to April so that was a really good chunk of work on offer. It was too good to turn down so the 1970s were off to a flying start.

Chapter 5

Laughs, More Laughs – But Some Tears Too

It was in April of 1970, still at the start of the new decade, that Barry and I started rehearsals in Leeds at the City Varieties. I'll never forget that first day and neither will Barry, it changed his entire life.

We walked on stage to meet everyone and start work when Barry noticed that he knew one of the dancers. It was Anne whom we had met the previous summer when she was dancing with a pal in a show at Rhyl. She was no longer part of the double act as she wanted to try her luck at being the lead girl in a troupe of six girl dancers. The dancers in those days got about £6 a week so it was okay to have a troupe of them. Nowadays you get two or three at most unless they are from a dance school and performing to get experience.

As arranged, we performed in Leeds for about six weeks before moving to Skegness in June for the summer season. That's where I took up golf for the first time. I bought an old set from Kenny Cantor who was the son of Terry and a very funny man in his own right. He was top of the bill in the show and his catchphrase was "Oh, you are kind". I remember that at the end of his act he used to say to the audience: "When I get home tonight my little boy will stand up in his cot and ask me what the audience was like. I will tell him you were a very good audience. Then he'll ask me that when I said goodnight did they jump up and down and cheer for more? I will say, 'of course they did son', and he will go to sleep happy. So, not for me ladies and gentlemen but for my son, I bid you goodnight."

It always worked for him, every single show.

The clubs Kenny sold me were from the 1930s, I think. They had wooden shafts! They did the trick though because they made me feel like a real golfer. I proudly turned up at the North Shore Golf Club in Skegness trying my best to look as if I had been playing for years. The other golfers didn't really look at me, they were too busy looking at my antique clubs.

I started and I had taken about nine shots and travelled no more than a hundred yards when the club secretary called me back and told me that I would have to learn to play a little before I could be let loose on the course. No one had told me that previously. I saw his point. On that day I could have scared the stripes off Tiger Woods!

After that I started to practice properly and then about halfway through the season I bought another set of clubs, a full set with all the extra bits. They were second-hand Ben Hogan Slazengers but at least they didn't look like they had been valued on the *Antiques Road Show*. I got on well with them and played with those clubs for many years.

I don't want to turn this into a golf book but I must tell you that I didn't manage to break one hundred until the following season when we were back in North Wales. I found out that my grip was all wrong, but that took some time to discover. In fact it was not until 1975 when we were in Jersey for the summer season. Tommy Horton was resident professional at the Royal Jersey Golf Club and he was also Ryder Cup Captain so he knew a thing or two about golf.

One night he came to see us at the Hawaiian Bar, Portelet Bay where we were in summer season. We had a drink with him after the show and he said he loved our act. I told him that I had started to play golf at his club and he invited me for a round with him. I thought all my birthdays had come at once.

I took him at his word and while we were playing he commented on my "cricket bat" grip and told me to come for a few free lessons. I was chuffed to bits and the next morning I turned up for my lesson. Tommy was as good as his word again and that summer my handicap fell from ten to seven. He was a great teacher as well as a great golfer.

There was another special moment on the golf course when I was playing the fifth hole which was right by the beach. I had made quite a good tee-shot and I was just getting my club ready for my second shot when I noticed that Tommy was putting on the green next to me. I waited for him, which is the right thing to do in golf etiquette, and then I realised who he was playing with. It was Tony Jacklin who had just won the Open and was already a golf legend. He nodded for me to take my shot and so I prepared myself really nervously because I was being watched by two of the greatest names in British golf. I took my swing and hit the ball perfectly. It flew like an arrow and landed about five feet from the pin. I was relieved and delighted but even more thrilled when Tony Jacklin said: "Good shot, son."

Imagine that, Tony Jacklin giving me a verbal pat on the back! I shouldn't go on about golf but that's how the game gets you.

I suppose some people are like that with cars and, talking of cars, Barry and I had shared a car for a number of years until after the pantomime at Sunderland when Barry took over our car for himself and took over the payments as well. I bought myself a second-hand Ford Anglia with the cut-away rear window. I remember it well because it was yellow with a white roof and a flash along the side. The bottom of the doors could hardly be seen for rust and there was a fair bit of rust in other places too. Since I had worked on bodywork and respraying at Harrison's it was not a problem for me to do it up a bit and by the time I had finished it was the best Anglia on the road. I resprayed it red and white – Rotherham United colours – put three spotlights on the front and turned the seating into jet black with some special upholstery paint. What a car it was!

Of course, now we both had cars and we thought we were the cat's whiskers. Looking back it just shows how daft you can be when you are young. On the road to Skegness, for instance, we thought it was great fun to keep on overtaking each other and then slowing down for the other one to overtake again. Stupid really, but we were young.

The show was at a kind of open air theatre behind the Embassy. In that summer show one of our routines was to appear as vicars. We marched on stage to the tune of *Come and Join Us* with a large bible each in our hands. The music stopped when we reached the microphone in centre stage then we would just stand there, deadpan, looking at the audience until someone would either laugh or say something like "Get on with it!" That is exactly what we were waiting for because we would both look directly at the person who had made the noise and frown at them with a kind of "How dare you" expression. That always got a laugh.

I would then open my book very slowly and carefully while Barry looked at me disdainfully. I would give a cough as if I was going to start reading and then do nothing. Barry would then give a high-pitched cough, open his book and blow talcum powder from it as if it was very dusty, and so it would go on. It was a routine that we had used a lot and seemed to get more laughs from doing very little than if we launched into a gag attack.

While we were at Skegness Embassy there were other shows in town. On the pier there was a guy playing bass in the band, who we got to know. He went on to other things in the business and eventually became our manager. It's funny how such things happen in this business. Who would have thought that Phil Dale, a bass-playing Manchester United fan in a summer season at Skegness, would eventually become the Chuckle Brothers manager?!

Anyway, Barry and Anne were seeing more and more of each other off the stage and eventually he popped the question. She accepted, poor girl. They married in the September, by which time we had finished the summer season and had returned to the City Varieties in Leeds for the later run of the same show.

Barry and Anne were hitched at the Registry Office in Rotherham and I was the best man. It's a good job we were not the Chuckle Brothers at that time. Can you imagine when I passed him the ring: "To Me… To You…." The reception was at Mum and Dad's house on Lockwood Close but we had a show to do at the City Varieties that evening so it didn't go on too long. All the company came over for the wedding because they felt they had been there from the very start, which they were. It was a great day and Barry and Anne are still together after all these years.

Not long after the autumn season we were rehearsing for

the pantomime which was to keep us at the City Varieties until April. It was *Little Red Riding Hood* and even though we have been in pantos every year since, we have never been in that panto again. We enjoyed it though, a long season and good audiences.

Kenny Cantor topped the bill, we were the village idiots (I know what you are thinking!!) and there was a girl playing Little Red Riding Hood who was really great. She was eighteen and only about 4'6" tall but packed with talent. I'm sorry, my love, but I don't remember your name. If you are out there though, you were a star.

We also worked and shared a dressing room with a singer called John Warwick. We asked him what he did and he told us he was a tenor. Yes, you've guessed it, we said we asked him what he did, not what he got paid! Despite that he put up with us for the full run of the panto.

Decimal coins came out that year and everyone was still trying to work out the price of everything in both new money and old money. Everything seemed more expensive, with one new penny being the equivalent of two and a half old pennies. We used to be able to get four chews for an old penny but when it changed we didn't get ten chews for a new penny. Not a chance. We could get four chews for a half-pence so they went up by about 50 per cent without anyone noticing. We noticed though. We were grumpy old men when we were young men!

The only downside of that panto season was on Saturdays when we had four shows to do. The first was at ten thirty in the morning and then we were given lunch in the circle bar before the next show at two o'clock. By the time we had finished that we were on our knees and still had two more shows to do. Our Dad had drummed into us that if we were tired it was not the audience's fault so still give them 100 per cent. We did of course and always have done. Somehow we used to get through the five o'clock performance and by the time the eight o'clock show started we were all on a high because we knew we were almost there.

After the show the night was young and I was only 23. Barry went home to his missus and I was staying in a rented house in Leeds with five girl dancers who all wanted to go out on the town. Oh to have that energy now! I am exhausted just writing this book!

The panto finished on April 15th and on the 18th we started rehearsals for our summer season at Prestatyn Holiday Camp. Of course our arrangements were different now. I had to find myself digs and Barry had to find digs for Anne and himself. I think I had the easier task. As it happens the park let me have one of the chalets on the site so it worked out really well for me and I had a ball over the season.

Once again we only performed on Friday night and Sunday nights so it was like going on a long holiday and I had time with various mates that I met. One of them was Keith Humphries whose parents owned a luxury caravan on the camp and owned a string of supermarkets in the Black Country. John's dad was also chairman of Stoke City, a role that Keith later took himself. Keith and I played table tennis for hours on end. He was brilliant and played for his county. After a couple of months our table tennis used to draw quite a crowd to watch us play. I used to stand about thirty feet back from the table and Keith would smash the ball at me for me to return and then we would change and I would do the smashing. It was great fun and seemed to entertain the crowds.

Keith had his 17th birthday while we were there and passed his driving test just a few days later. His dad bought him a brand new Ford Capri 1600, a superb car. On the Saturday he took me to see Stoke City play away to Coventry. On the motorway he was soon doing ninety miles an hour. I noticed that he was still in third gear and mentioned it. "I wondered why it wouldn't go faster," he said and the next thing I knew he had changed gear and we were now doing 120 mph!

We went all over the place that summer, Chester Races, golf and even a trip to his dad's house just outside Stoke. I call it a house but it was a mansion, of which his dad was very proud. I had never seen anything like it. It had a long drive, its own lake, stables, gardens, the whole lot and inside it was full of the most beautiful furniture. It was fantastic and all the more so because only six years earlier Keith's dad was a market trader and going to work on the bus.

Of course, I thought my car caught the eye of the girls but nothing like Keith's Capri. What a summer that was, the girls were....

Oh all right Sue, I'll leave it there.

One of our other pastimes was playing tennis and one particular day we had been playing in the sun and I had not realised how strong it was. When I took my tee-shirt off you wouldn't have known that I had taken it off. My arms, neck and face were brilliant Post Office red while my torso was pure white.

During the show we were doing a routine which we still do today. I had to enter stage without a shirt and see Barry wearing my shirt and demand it off him. Two others had already been on stage and demanded that he give them back their jacket and trousers. When I entered with my very white, bare, skinny chest – I was very skinny in those days, 5ft 11ins and nine stone soaking wet – the audience just exploded with laughter because I looked like a raspberry ripple.

That was not the end of it either. Instead of laughing as

well, Barry looked really worried. He was supposed to be left standing there wearing just some frilly pants but as he turned his back to the audience to remove the shirt he whispered to me that he had forgotten to put the pants on. As a result he would be left with just a pair of old Y-fronts (clean ones I'm pleased to say). We went through with it, though I couldn't stop laughing. Barry was left to face the audience with his hands hiding his Y-fronts.

That still wasn't the end of it. A girl was supposed to dash on after me and demand her frilly knickers back. She ran on, not knowing that Barry wasn't wearing the knickers but she chased him off anyway after demanding the Y-fronts. It was hysterical!

We still use many of the gags that we used to use and many of them came from our Dad who used them long before us. They are not exactly the same gags because times and audiences change but the ideas are often the same and the laughter they get is still definitely the same. The gags change as we change as well.

I don't look skinny now like I used to. Barry is as skinny as ever which I think is down to the food he eats. He still doesn't like curries or anything like that. He is a roast beef and Yorkshire pudding man, or egg and chips, that kind of thing. I will eat almost anything except most fish dishes. I like fish and chips but I can't be doing with turbot or lobster.

I believe it stems back to when I was little and Mum would take us to the market in Rotherham. For some unknown reason she seemed to always leave us near the fish stall while she did some shopping. I can see and smell it now, water dripping off the white marble on which all kinds of dead fish were laid out. Since then I have never liked fish unless it is disguised in batter.

What I did like about the market was the mushy pea stall. You could get a bowl of mushy peas with mint sauce and a spoon. That was really superb, a lot better than today's so-called fast food chains.

Nowadays I do a lot of cooking which is why probably why I have put on a bit of weight. I worked out any food can taste good as long as it is well salted, has a lot of butter or cream and you enjoy putting it together. I find preparing vegetables very therapeutic. I spend many a happy hour preparing food with just my own company.

Try this simple little starter. Dice chicken into bite sizes and sauté until browned. Take out of the pan and put to one side. Put pan back on to heat and add half a glass of white wine. This will release the sediment from the bottom of the pan. Now add two teaspoons of English mustard, a couple of knobs of butter and mix well. Put the chicken back into the pan and coat with the sauce. Now add a cup of double cream until simmering, then serve. Believe me, it's gorgeous.

I bet no one expected a food recipe in this book!

At the end of our summer season we were back on the social club circuit. We had been appearing at quite a few places on the North Wales coast during the summer for some extra 'dosh'. We were really looking forward to the panto season because we were going to be in Barnsley which meant that we could stay at home at Christmas. It was at Barnsley that I met my first wife, Anna. It wasn't one of those whirlwind things. We just sort of drifted into it during the next few months.

When we finished our season at Barnsley we went straight into the last couple of weeks of another panto at the Alhambra Theatre in Bradford. An act called Lester and Smart had been in the panto but they had to leave early to go to an engagement in Australia. Barry and I took over and we just clicked with the audience and the management who promptly booked us for the following year's pantomime, the 1972-73 season.

For the summer season we were booked at Skegness again, this time actually inside the old Embassy Theatre, not the theatre you see now of course, but the one that used to be on the same site. It was like a dance hall with a stage but for a theatre setting there were rows of chairs put out and it did have quite a music hall feel about the place – maybe it was its age. Today of course the Embassy is a modern theatre with many more seats and great facilities. We go there regularly with the Chuckle Brothers show and always enjoy it.

Anna got herself a season with the dance troupe at Butlins just down the road so we rented a bungalow from June to September and it was in that September we got married at the Spilsby Registry Office. At the end of the season we moved back to Maltby and lived with my Mum and Dad.

To be honest, we couldn't really afford to get married let alone find a home of our own but we were young and thought it would all work out for the best. It is funny how we all think we are wise when we are still in our early 20s and have all the answers. Still, at least it was Anna who had to live with her mother-in-law, not me. Having said that, my mother-in-law was really nice. In fact, if she lived in India she'd have been sacred!

I managed to get Anna in the chorus at Bradford so that we could work together throughout the panto season. The panto was *Aladdin* and Barry and I were the Chinese policemen. We were thrilled to bits when we read the review in The Stage. It said: "If there's a funnier double act in the country working pantomime today, I've yet to see it." That was the best critique we had received in ten years of performing and it felt great. I think we must have read those words over and over about fifty times before we put the paper down for a while.

The Alhambra is one of the finest theatres in the land outside London and one of the best to work in. Back in that 1972-73 season the lighting grid was at the side of the stage. It was a massive grid of wheels and handles and adjusted the lights on stage. That is about the only time we ever saw a lighting grid like that. Usually they are out front. Of course, all the lighting is computerised these days.

"Diddy" David Hamilton was top of the bill in the pantomime and we did a couple of gags with him, one of which involved him almost getting a large plateful of ice cream in his face. He never actually got hit with it of course, try as we might. Well, that is not totally true. David was very meticulous about his appearance, especially his golden hair, so we were very careful not to accidentally splat him.

Of course on the last performance of a panto season the script does tend to go out of the window and the crew and staff all asked me to get David with the ice cream. It was not that he was disliked. In fact, he was a really nice guy and we had the pleasure of working with him again in variety shows later. It was just that everyone wanted to see his hair get messed up.

I remember him looking at me with a wary glint in his eye. He tried to pre-empt my movements but in the end I pre-empted him and he got it full in the face. The gag got a bigger laugh than ever because the audience sensed what was going on and they were certainly joined by the band and the rest of the crew.

The panto season ran until the end of February, after which we returned once again to the club circuit. That had not been going for long when Anna and I had a surprise, courtesy of a pregnancy test. Yes, there was a baby on the way. The surprise was that Anna had been on the pill so we were not expecting that she would be expecting, if you see what I mean.

Living with my Mum and Dad was not the ideal situation

with a baby on the way but we were still looking forward to the event which we learned was likely to be in October. I kind of hoped it would be on the 18th as that would be the same birthday as me. Anyway that was still seven months away and there was another summer season at Skegness to do.

This time we were at the Derbyshire Miners Holiday Centre and part of their theatre show. Some acts were for their cabaret room but we were theatre which meant that we had a couple of days off each week. That was just as well as it happened because Anna and I bought a cheap caravan for the season to save money but she could not live in it comfortably so she went back to live with her mother in Maltby and I went there during my days off so that I could go with her to the various clinics for pregnant ladies.

It was a good summer season though, I even managed to get my golf handicap down to 21! I loved playing the North Shore course at Skegness, probably my favourite golf course of all time, which has something to do with my best round of all time. It was in 1977 and I was a man on a mission that day, hitting just about every shot perfectly. Eventually I was standing on the 18th and final tee with a card showing one under par. I only had to make par and I would have been celebrating. It was around three hundred yards and I had previously birdied it a dozen or more times and even eagled it at least twice. I was fairly confident that I could get on the green with one and then hopefully with a couple of putts to sink it for three and a birdie.

I gave a lot of thought to which club I should use. That was a mistake, I should have just picked one and hit it. No, I had to have a long debate with myself and I just couldn't make my mind up. In the end I decided upon the No 3 wood and I hit it. It was not bad, long and straight and about seventy yards short of the green. I can still get near the hole from here, I thought. So

I hit it again with the No 7 iron and it landed about three yards short of the green. I did not believe that I had played such a poor shot and told myself off in words that cannot be printed in this book.

My next shot took me to within three feet of the hole and then I putted and the ball stopped two inches short of the hole. My birdie turned into a bogey and I finished on par for the course. It was still a good round for an amateur but I really thought I was going to finish like a champion. Another below par performance but not in the right way!

We also played football at least once a week, the entertainers against the kitchen staff. The football pitch was about three quarters of the size of the usual but it was still like Wembley to us. Barry played his usual position on the right wing and I was the striker in the middle. There were no offsides and there were about seven on each side so there were sure to be plenty of goals. Our defence was pretty solid and they just booted the ball up to me and I had only the goalkeeper to beat. I think we invented the long direct ball tactic. I scored five or six goals every game so I was not just a star golfer but also a star footballer. Is there no end to this man's talents?!

The panto season soon came round and we were booked into Swinton in Manchester but before then there was a big role to play as I was about to become a dad for the first time. We were still going for the regular checks of course and we were a bit surprised during September to be told that the baby was likely to arrive in November. Prior to that we had believed it would be October but now we were being told that the size of the baby meant that it was going to be the end of November. Then we were told that it was going to a Christmas baby.

That didn't really make sense to us as it would have meant that Anna would have had an eleven-month pregnancy!

Anyway, you can't argue about these things. They agreed though that if Anna had not gone into labour before the end of November they would induce the baby.

The day before the deadline they had set, Anna did go into labour. It was a long 24-hour job and there was a complication because Anna's waters had dried. We believe that it had been caused by the delay. They moved her from the maternity home to Rotherham General Hospital because Anna's blood pressure and temperature had gone sky high. Needless to say it was a really nail-biting time for all of us. Eventually our beautiful and petite little girl, Nicola, was born, weighing in at just 5lbs. Within 24 hours she was at home with us in Maltby and all was well.

Barry and I started the panto at the beginning of December when Nicola was just a few days old. After a few weeks she started to develop a bit of a tummy on her but my mother said this is often normal in a small baby. It was a bit of a worry though. When we took her for her six weeks check-up we asked the doctor about it. He had a good look and feel and sent us to Manchester Children's Hospital, which is one of the best in the country. The staff were brilliant and gave her a thorough examination and then asked if they could keep her in for observation. Since it was Friday afternoon she would stay in for the weekend but we could spend as much time there as we wanted.

That Friday evening's panto performance was one of the most difficult I have ever had to do. Making people laugh when your own stomach is churning is difficult to say the least. I could not get my little angel out of my mind but, as they say in our business "The show must go on" and it does, even in the most difficult of circumstances. The audience is there to be entertained like any other show and deserves the best.

Monday came and went and Nicola was still in hospital. They couldn't actually find what was wrong except that she was anaemic and needed a blood transfusion. They have different methods now, of course. They decided to keep her in until they found out what was really wrong.

The panto season ended and we had to return to Rotherham. We could only afford to go and see her every other day which was a heartbreak all of its own. We wanted our little girl home with us of course.

A month after the panto ended, Barry and I were booked by an agent to do two weeks in the Edinburgh area. I phoned home every evening to see how Anna and Nicola were and we were three days into our run when I phoned home as usual and Anna could hardly speak to me. Nicola had passed away that afternoon.

The thought that she could actually die had never been mentioned. Perhaps I buried my head in the sand, I don't know, but I would never wish that news or that feeling on anyone. I thought I would never get over the sick hurting in my stomach. Time does heal of course... sort of. Nicola would have been forty now and I recently went to her grave and found that the hurt came back instantly, with floods of tears for my little girl.

The funeral was set for the following Wednesday when Barry and I were still in Scotland. I had to go cap-in-hand to the agent to ask for the time off. He said that we were not booked for the Tuesday so that was not a problem but we were booked for the Wednesday evening and we would have to honour that engagement or lose all the pay for the entire fortnight. We pleaded with him but he wouldn't budge and we couldn't afford to just walk away.

Can you imagine what it was like? Just thirty minutes after throwing the earth on Nicola's coffin and saying goodbye to my little girl, we were back on the road to Edinburgh to work a club. I had to leave my grieving wife and all the family at home. I should have told the agent what to do with his engagement at the time but we really could not afford to lose the money.

It was a most awful time. I should have been at home hugging my wife and sharing our tears but instead we had to complete the last few days of the Edinburgh fortnight because we couldn't be released from the last few days of our contract.

Chapter 6

The Show Must Go On

The next few months were just a blur really, except that we auditioned for *New Faces*, a very popular TV talent show of the 1970s and we were told that we would be appearing at some time.

Our summer season promised to be something different as we were booked into the Tower Circus at Blackpool. I got Anna a job in the box office as we didn't want to be apart and she needed something to take her mind off things. We had never done circus before but learned a lot from the experience of working with the legendary clown Charlie Cairoli.

Our job was to do the run-ins which were to cover the removal of props and so on. Yes, we wore red noses and did short routines of the sort you would probably have seen. In one I balanced a broom handle on my head with a tray on top of it. Barry would then run in and grab the broom handle which meant that the tray then fell down onto my head and I would chase him out.

The big comedy routine of the show starred Charlie of course and came near the end of the performance. We were asked to take part in that. Barry and I came out and started doing *Singing in the Rain*. Then we stopped and complained to the ringmaster that we had been promised special effects of rain and our performance was being ruined by the lack of it. We did our best to sound like prima donnas and said that if Gene Kelly could have rain then we should have rain.

The ringmaster then called for Charlie Cairoli – the maintenance man – and we had a go at him. It was always hard trying to look serious because just looking at Charlie made you laugh. He only had to raise one eyebrow and you were in hysterics. Charlie had a mug of tea in his hand and passed it to Barry to hold while I was telling him off. Every time Charlie looked away Barry took a sip of the tea and, of course, Charlie kept on doing double-takes. The audience loved it but we had only just started.

Charlie's stooge, Jimmy, then entered. Jimmy worked with Charlie for years and was totally brilliant. He never really spoke because he didn't do words but his facial expressions and movements more than made up for it. Charlie Cairoli Jnr then also came into the act as an extra pair of hands.

Jimmy set up some step ladders and sat on top with a bucket of water. The music started again and we tried once again with *Singing in the Rain*. We danced away from the step ladder so Charlie waved to Jimmy to get down and move the ladders, which he did with just a little bit of sloshing of water. No sooner had he set up the ladders and got to the top again than we danced to another part of the ring so that he poured water onto nothing.

We stopped the music again and complained that there was still no rain while we were singing. Charlie came over to us and said: "Oh, it's water you want."

"That's what I keep telling you," I replied. "Give us some water."

Charlie then pulled a knowing face at the audience, shrugged his shoulders and said: "Well, if it's water you want, it's water you'll get."

We started singing and dancing again and Jimmy and Charlie Jnr reappeared along with half a dozen ring boys and threw buckets of water over us. Charlie came back on with a hosepipe and finished the job off, making sure he swished a little over the audience too.

While all of this was going on, the ring started to descend for the Tower Circus finale which is always a big water spectacular with fountains and a pool, famous throughout the world actually. As the ring descended we carried on singing until we were up to our waists.

It was a great routine, but unknown to the audience Jimmy was a bit of a prankster and sometimes he would prepare a bucket of water that was icy cold to throw at us. It was a great laugh though and he was always there to help us out of the water at the end of the routine. He hated water himself and was always the first one out. Charlie joked that the last time Jimmy was in water his mum was bathing him in the sink.

We did get our own back on Jimmy though, as one day when he was helping us out of the water we pulled him in head first. He almost bounced back out as he was so keen to get away from the water. He never threw icy water at us again!

Charlie Cairoli Jnr became a good friend and he and his wife, Claudie, are a great couple of people. You don't meet many really genuine friends in this life but they are among the best. He has been through some heavy medical stuff during the past few years but Charlie has never lost his sense of humour or thoughtfulness towards others, a great guy just like his late father.

Charlie Snr used to tell us some fantastic stories, like the time he went fishing, which was one of his favourite pastimes. He told us of the time he went out and found a lovely pond on a farm. He called at the farmhouse door to ask if he would be allowed to fish in the pond. The second the farmer saw who he was there was no way he was going to refuse as he was a huge fan.

Charlie liked to be all on his own when he was fishing and the farmer assured him that no one would come anywhere near him. Charlie started to bait his rods with worms when suddenly there was a great commotion behind him. He turned round to find that a chicken had taken a fancy to one of the worms he had already put on his line.

Of course, the chicken had taken the hook as well as the worm and was squawking and going on. Charlie reeled it in but didn't know what to do. He was not going to be able to get the hook out of the chicken. He didn't want to call for help and upset the farmer so he saw only one option. He quickly killed the chicken and stuffed it in his bag.

As it happened he did not catch one fish but when he got home and his wife asked how he had got on, he took the chicken out of his bag and said: "I caught a big, fat, juicy hen!"

Charlie was brilliant entertainment both in and out of the ring and we never tired of working with him or listening to the many great stories of his travels and experiences in the world of circus.

While we were with the Blackpool circus there were animals in the show. The programme included lions, elephants, horses, dogs and sea lions. The only ones we were warned not to go near was the sea lions who had very sharp teeth and would take your arm off if given the chance.

The lions were fine, born in captivity and used to people. They were more like family pets although I would not have fancied going in the cage with them myself and I certainly wouldn't have one sitting on my lap while I watched TV.

We were warned not to get too close to the elephants either. They were a bit unpredictable. In one performance one of them tried to impose herself on their great trainer John Gindl, an older German trainer with a wealth of experience. He made the mistake of walking behind one of them and the elephant promptly sat on him.

Everyone scrambled to try and get the elephant off him but unless you have tried it I suppose you could never know how difficult it is to move several tons of elephant when it doesn't want to go anywhere. It took about five minutes to persuade her to stand up and when she did we were all relieved to see John Gindl emerge virtually unscathed and with a smile on his face. John was about seventy and had worked with elephants and horses all his life. He even smelled like an elephant! He knew exactly what to do as the elephant sat on him and rolled under what he called her soft parts. It was not a nice thought but his knowledge and experience saved his life. We kept away from the elephants after that.

During that summer of 1974 the World Cup was on and we rigged about a hundred yards of aerial cable so that we could have the TV on in our dressing room. It took ages to rig partly up the Tower, down air shafts and all over the place, but the outcome was that we got a perfect picture. Since there were about ten different nationalities in the show everyone had a team and the World Cup was something we all shared.

A number of us shared golf as well. Barry had taken it up by now and we played regularly, along with some of the other entertainers in the show and from other shows in Blackpool that year. One Swedish guy actually had a handicap of one. If he had not liked circus so much he could have been a professional golfer!

Val Doonican was in a show in Blackpool and we played together a few times. What a nice man and a very good golfer. I remember playing with him one day and my glove was in tatters. He noticed, took out a bag of about fifty new gloves and gave me a couple. He told he was sponsored by Dunlop who kept sending him stuff.

We had a golf competition every Thursday morning at Stanley Park Golf Course and I would run a book on it. I would give odds on all the players and would give very good odds on Gert, our Swedish friend. Everyone knew he was the best player so they would put their money on him. It wasn't much of a chance as he had to give loads of shots to everyone. I never lost money all season and my golf handicap came down again as I was playing really well.

Val Doonican invited me to play in a tournament challenge at Royal St Lytham against a US Army Sergeants team. It was the day after the Open had finished there and all the stands were still up so it was an extra thrill to be playing the course as if we were part of the Open. The Americans beat us but since their handicap system was different to ours, we probably gave a good account of ourselves and certainly enjoyed the day.

Since this is starting to sound like a book of golf memories. I'll apologise to non-golfers and get on with the rest of the Chuckle Brothers story.

The Blackpool season closed at the end of October and we were going into pantomime at Bournemouth. In between we made our *New Faces* appearance on December 4th and we were delighted to see that the panel of judges, which included Clifford Henry, the great Ted Ray and Mickie Most, were laughing at our gags at the rehearsal and we just hoped that the actual show would go as well. It did. We got the highest marks from the panel, great reaction from the audience and even the camera crew laughed. At the end of the show we joined in with the theme music and hoped that this was our really big breakthrough.

We did get a good reaction from viewers and everyone else we came into contact with after that show. The following Monday we began rehearsals for the Bournemouth panto which had Dickie Henderson and Arthur Askey topping the bill.

We were contacted by ATV again who wanted us to appear on the *New Faces All Winners Show* at the end of December but we couldn't do it because we were committed to the panto until the end of February. So they put us into the March final instead and told us that we had received the biggest viewers vote yet, which was great news of course.

Unfortunately our then manager made a mistake and booked us into Jersey for a season of 22 weeks. It was brilliant to have a nice long season in a beautiful place but the trouble was that it took us out of circulation in England for the best part of six months at a time when we should have been cashing in on our *New Faces* success. In fact we were offered to appear in a TV summer show every Saturday but the man we were working for in Jersey, Chris Savva, would not let us out of the contract for two days a week so that had to be turned down.

Then we were offered the Lulu TV show every week but that had to be turned down as well, so in effect we became hot property but quickly cooled off because we were not available for six months. When we were available the attention had gone and we had to wait another eight years before getting another big TV chance.

We had a good season in Jersey though and learned to surf with help from a mate and fellow performer Andy Mann, Andy Beaumont as he was known off stage. Getting me surfing was quite an achievement as I couldn't even swim when I first went to Jersey. Sadly Andy died a few years ago as the result of a brain tumour.

I have already talked about the golf exploits in Jersey so I won't go through that again except to say that I won several competitions.

We also played football every Wednesday. Our team included the popular Liverpool group The Fourmost as well as a singer named Brian. Sorry mate, I can't recall your other name but you were a brilliant footballer. Brian had been on Tottenham's books but they let him go. We were getting a bit of a reputation as a strong team and the local paper reported our matches. In the end we were challenged by the Guernsey national team to play them in a charity match. They slaughtered us but about 5,000 people turned up to watch so we enjoyed it and so did the charities it helped.

When we travelled over to Jersey in the first place I felt sick as a dog. It was a hot day and the sea was so calm that it looked like a mill pond. Sitting inside the boat though there was still the sight of the horizon going up and down and I kept trying not to look. In the end I couldn't stand it any longer and had to go upstairs to get some fresh air. I felt heartily sick on a calm day.

When we were due to travel back at the end of the season the weather forecast was for a force eight gale. We were told that if it reached force nine the ferries would be cancelled. It didn't and they weren't, although we wished that it had and they hadn't, if you see what I mean.

As it happens we really enjoyed it. The front end of the boat was rising about forty or fifty feet in the air and then crashing down onto the surf with a bang. We walked to the restaurant by taking two steps uphill and then running forward as the front end dropped. The eggs were sliding back and forth on the platter, as were the sausages and boiled tomatoes. Not many people were eating that day but Barry and I ate loads and never once felt the slightest bit queezy although we had both felt so dreadful when the sea was calm.

That Christmas we were in *Aladdin* again, this time at the Norwich Theatre Royal with John Inman topping the bill. It was perfect timing for the theatre management as John was appearing in *Are You Being Served* on television and the programme really took off, especially with John's character, Mr Humphreys, and his catch phrase "I'm Free!" being shrilled by everyone all over the country. John was good to work with but a little unhappy that his own management had not got him better money as he had become a national star. The trouble was that the deal had been done before the show had proved to be a big hit so it was a bit of a gamble for all concerned.

The theatre was packed for every performance and we got to know the manager, Dick Condon, who became a legend in show business. When he took over the venue he transformed it and had people flocking from miles away to see the shows he put on there.

He told us a little story of a local councillor who came to the theatre on the opening night of a show not long after a new carpet costing £30,000 had been fitted throughout the venue. The place was heaving with people and the councillor complained that if Dick kept getting so many people into the theatre the carpet would soon have to be replaced again and the council could not expect to keep on buying carpets! Dick could hardly believe his ears that a councillor was complaining about the theatre being successful.

There was a lot of snow that winter and we were staying in a cottage on a farm just outside Norwich. More than once we had to ask the farmer to help get us on the road to the theatre for performances. He was always very helpful though and never complained.

We enjoyed the panto as we always do when playing to packed houses. Dick Condon was a genius in picking the right shows, marketing them properly and keeping the theatre at the focus of public attention. A really great theatre man.

Of course the year ended while we were at Norwich and we had no summer show to look forward to at that stage. We had wasted our success on *New Faces* and it was almost like starting all over again. In a sense we did, because we parted company with our manager and once again had to fend for ourselves with nothing in the diary.

I turned to taxi driving for six months. That was in 1976 when some of you might recall that it was hotter than hot. I mostly did night shifts which meant starting at about seven in the evening and taking people into town for their drinks, meals and so on. It would go quiet at about half past eight for the best part of two hours and then it would start again until after midnight with all those people wanting to be taken home. One advantage is that people often tipped more than they would have done if they had not been drinking. Perhaps that's word the word 'tipsy' comes from!

I did really well financially and after three months I bought a second car and started getting other drivers to taxi for me. That was a big mistake. Within two weeks I worked out that the extra car was doing about twelve miles to the gallon instead of thirty.

The other drivers were filling it up and putting some in cans for themselves.

There were other incidents, like people taking the car home and then not turning up for work for several days, that kind of thing. What was a decent business started to turn into a nightmare and I could not wait for the panto season to come round and head for Wolverhampton. Oh well, you learn by your mistakes – at least some people seem to. I just seem to make different mistakes!

Don Maclean, then of *Crackerjack!* fame (CRACKERJACK!), was top of the bill at Wolverhampton with the little-known Sue Pollard – soon to become a comedy star – as the Dame and with Anne Aston from TV's *The Golden Shot* playing the Princess.

One day during rehearsals the director of the Grand Theatre told us, that is Don, Barry and me, that he had this fabulous comedy set for us, one that took up the whole of the stage. We couldn't wait to go and see it. He was right, it was massive and looked great. It was like a big steam engine with lots of wheels and cogs.

"What does it do?" We asked him.

He looked at us rather blankly and said: "You're the comedians, surely you can think of something?"

We were totally flabbergasted and could not believe that he had spent all that money on a fantastic prop without knowing what it was supposed to do or without having some routine in mind. Still, we got on with it and created what turned out to be a very funny routine which involved it dispensing all sorts of things including a pint of green liquid which we called Night Nurse because that particular product was being advertised all over the place.

It ended up with the machine giving out a squawk and

laying what was supposed to be a large egg but was actually an inflated balloon filled with foam. The pay-off to the whole thing was Don 'cracking' the egg over my head so that I ended up with a hat covered in foam. The audience loved it and it worked especially well since Barry and I then walked forward, allowing the front cloth to drop behind us and the villain then walk on from the side.

We always love to play along with the bad guy in pantomime because he's the one you can get the most laughs out of. The audience hates him and he gets no sympathy, so we can do what we like. Some little kids are scared of him so they like it when he gets taken down a peg by us.

In this routine he walked on as Barry and I were standing there, me with my hat covered in foam. As I turned round quickly some of the foam would fly off and hit the villain in the face. The audience loved it.

The funniest routine we did at Wolverhampton was one we still sometimes use today. It was a routine The Pirates used to do years before. It involved two wires hanging from the grid and fastened to a harness worn by Don. The light was very low, with ultra violet light picking us out on stage. I would lift Don off the ground, holding his hands and lifting him straight up above my head. This always gets shocked laughter as it looks so impossible. Then comes the extra laugh as Barry would then come in and take hold of my ankles and appear to lift me up so Barry was actually holding both of us.

We had a lot of fun with this routine and the band especially loved it because we came out dressed as different characters every night. Tonight we might be German Stormtroopers and tomorrow Japanese Kamikaze pilots.

Though we ad-libbed a lot with Don that season, the three of us got on like a house on fire. One day in the middle of a scene,

Don put his arm round Barry and said to the audience: "Look at him, ladies and gentlemen. Believe it or not he has been married seven times. Isn't that right?"

Barry, looking a little gormless, nodded his head and said: "Yes, that's right, seven times."

Don then said: "Take a proper look at him ladies and gentlemen – married seven times and he used to be a heavyweight weight-lifter!"

It was a total ad-lib – the sort of thing that often gets thrown into a script, especially in panto and it got a great laugh.

The first of computer game consoles was released that Christmas. All it did was play ping-pong from side to side. Two players had a paddle which you moved up and down the screen to hit the ball back the other way. It would be like a museum piece now but at the time it was quite mind-blowing. We had to have one and bought it for £50. Our thought was that if anyone wanted to play it, we could charge them 10p a time and get our money back – and we did!

The stage crew were the biggest players and we got back all but a fiver of our original outlay. When you add to that the pool tournament which I won (there was a table in the Green Room), the football lottery which I ran every Saturday, and our performance fees, it was not a bad season. We even found time for five-a-side football. It was certainly a memorable panto run for many different reasons.

The 1977 summer season saw us return to the Derbyshire Miners Holiday Centre in Skegness. I couldn't wait to get back to Skeggy, the golf, the football matches and everything else we enjoyed about our long season there.

Anna and I rented one of the caravan homes for the season. It had all we needed and while I was at Derbyshire Miners, Anna was engaged as a dancer with Duggie Chapman's Music Hall at the Embassy so it all worked out quite well really, with two wages coming in.

Among the highlights of that summer was having Ray Clemence playing in our football team. Ray was top goalkeeper with Liverpool and England at the time and since he came from Skegness originally he used to spend a couple of weeks of his summer break back there to be with family. He also liked to play golf at North Shore and we got talking and asked him to play for us. The kitchen staff agreed that he could be in our team as long as he didn't go in goal. So he played outfield and was just as brilliant there. In the first week he scored seven amazing goals and in the second week he topped that with nine goals. When he hit the ball it went like a rocket. Nobody would have stopped his shots – except perhaps himself!

I also recall that the amazing Tommy Cooper was appearing at the Skegness Pier Theatre that season and every day he would turn up at the North Shore Golf Club, get his clubs out of the boot, carry them into the hotel entrance and put them down before going into the bar and ordering a Scotch. At around five he would pick up his clubs, put them in the car and leave. I don't know if he ever actually played a round of golf, he never did when I was there, but what a lovely man he was, a huge talent of natural comedy.

There were five other golfers in that summer show at Derbyshire Miners and of course we had to start up a tournament. Each week's winner had their name engraved on the trophy. By the end of the season I had won it three times and Lance Fortune, a singer from the same stable as Adam Faith and others, had won it twice. So it was all down to the final game of the season. It went further because it was all down to the last putt on the last hole. Lance was getting more and more tense as the game went on but he had only to sink an eight inch putt to win the game and take the trophy to a play-off. He missed from just eight inches. I couldn't believe it, but the trophy still proudly stands behind my bar at home.

We did have some good times during those summer seasons as well as the panto seasons of course and when I think back to the words of my old headmaster, who said I would get nowhere in life unless I went into the steel or coal industries, well, with respect, he didn't know me very well and I'm glad I didn't listen to him.

It was back to Bournemouth Pavilion again for the 1977-78 season. Don Maclean had been booked and he stipulated that he wanted to work with us so that we could do some of the same routines which had worked so well before.

. Lenny Henry was in the show as well playing the Slave of the Lamp. It was his first panto and I think he enjoyed the experience. Also in the show playing the Dame was one of the nicest people I have ever met – Peter Butterworth. He was well known for his appearances in all the Carry On films but he was also a well-established entertainer in other comedy dramas, radio and even recordings.

At Bournemouth Peter was playing Widow Twankey and what a lovely man he was, now dearly missed of course. Not many people knew, we certainly didn't until he told us when we were chatting one day, but Peter flew Spitfires in the Second World War and took part in the Battle of Britain. He was actually shot down after that famous Battle and spent the rest of the war as a POW.

Evidently he had some shrapnel embedded very close to his heart, too close to be removed so he just lived with it and never let it stop him from being a very funny man.

Barry and I had a great routine going with the villain that year too. We were the Chinese policemen and during one scene with the villain, the bad guy would grab hold of Barry, shake him about a bit and then hold me with his face just inches from his own, all the time telling him off. I would tap Barry on the shoulder while the villain was holding him and say: "He can't talk to you like that."

Barry would then say to the villain: "You can't talk to me like that."

You can guess what's coming next. Yes, of course, the villain would say: "Oh yes I can!" Then the audience would join in until Barry would finally say: "Oh yes he can."

At one of the early performances, as Barry and the villain were doing the shaking about stuff, their hats fell off. They stopped and picked them up but each picked up the wrong hat and put them on. It brought the place down. The villain looked really funny with a massive flowing outfit and a little police helmet. It didn't end there because when the villain whipped the hat off he whipped off a toupee as well, revealing a bald head underneath. That also was a false one which he had obtained for another gag but it fitted perfectly with this one.

I lost the plot and could not stop laughing, the tears pouring down my face. The band also lost it and could not play for five minutes. It was one of those many special moments.

There used to be a cool night club in Bournemouth called Bumbles. The group of us often went there and enjoyed some relax time. I especially liked the music. I am into all sorts of music but in my car you will mostly find the music of the 80s, which I thought was a really good music era with The Human League, Annie Lennox, The Thompson Twins, Bronsky Beat, ABC and the rest. Great stuff!

I changed my car again that season. When I look back I must have wasted a fortune on changing my car. This one was a Ford Granada and I fell in love with it the moment I sat behind the wheel. I have always liked big cars and this one certainly lived up to that. Barry prefers small cars – well he would do. We are opposites in most things. I like a sunroof too, so the Granada ticked all the right boxes. The Granada even had reclining seats that turned into a double bed – what a car! I loved it.

The pantomime ended the beginning of March and we went back to the clubs again to earn a crust. What bit of money you have put to one side goes so fast when you are not earning. One thing about entertainers is that they are all optimists and they are all expecting that special phone call that will take them to their own TV series, a season at the Palladium or something that will be the next highlight of their career. Barry and I were no different.

Chapter 7

Ice Cream and a Vision

We struggled a bit to get a summer season that year. That happens sometimes for no particular reason. We ended up getting a touring season with Warners. Instead of being in one camp you go to several of them each week. My then wife, Anna, got a summer season at Gorleston near Great Yarmouth, working for Duggie Chapman again, so we rented a house for us there and Barry rented a caravan nearby so that his family could be by the coast for the summer.

It was as easy – or difficult – for us to be based there as it would have been at Rotherham as we were to appear at Warners camps at Great Yarmouth, Felixstowe, the Isle of Sheppey and two different camps on Hayling Island. If you look on a map you will see that it was a pretty hectic schedule with a lot of driving. That's the world of entertainment though, you can spend an awful lot of time – or a lot of awful time – on the road.

Most people seem to think that we have an easy life. You turn up at a venue, appear for about 45 minutes, pick up your money and go. It is not quite as simple as that though. Driving for hours, especially in the winter, to get to the venue and then breaking down on the way home is just part of the fun. With Barry and I being a double act we could always share the driving and the problems. Usually I drive to the gigs and Barry drives back. He is teetotal while I like a drink after the show. As I said, we are opposites. He doesn't like anything other than plain cooking while I like spicy and exotic food. He gets fed up after a short time on holiday while I could holiday for six months and never get bored.

At least we have one common love – Rotherham United. We go as often as we can and have followed the Millers through thick and thin. The new ground is fantastic and we have high hopes that one day soon it will be full every week for the visits of Manchester United, Arsenal and Liverpool when Rotherham are in the Premier League.

Actually I am also a very strong Liverpool fan but Rotherham United will always be my first love.

Get on with it, Paul!

The nights we worked at Hayling Island were also complete opposites. There were two camps – and what a contrast. The first night was at Coronation Camp and the audience was always brilliant. The second camp was called Northney and the venue was a massive ballroom with kids sliding all over the floor while we were on stage. This was before *ChuckleVision* so the kids had no idea who we were except for two daft men being silly on stage while they played. The acoustics were awful as well and we sounded like a couple of announcers at Kings Cross railway station. They only had one microphone so Barry and I had to share it and make sure we got our timing absolutely perfect. It was pretty awful really but, as they say, the show had to go on and we did our best. We used to finish at about half past ten and then drive back to Great Yarmouth, usually arriving in time to see the sun rising.

I remember one night we were treated to a thunder storm as we drove back and the sky was lit up when we were around Ipswich. The rain hammered down in a sheet so that we could not even see the end of the car. The wipers could barely cope with it and we had to crawl all the way. It was about seven in the morning when we finally arrived back in Yarmouth. Oh, the joys of a travelling summer season.

Warners put us up for the first night in one of their chalets in the Coronation Camp. That was nice until one day when we arrived we were told that the camp was full and there was no overnight accommodation for us. We asked the entertainments manager what we were supposed to do, especially since it was part of our contract. He just shrugged his shoulders and said it wasn't his problem.

As I said before, my Ford Granada provided us with a double bed, so that would have to do. It was parked in the middle of the camp and we always carried blankets and so on in case of emergencies. The show went really well once again and after a bag of chips we went to sleep in the car. The next morning all hell broke loose. When the campers saw that we had been forced to sleep in the car overnight they were up in arms and complained that we had been shabbily treated. They didn't really do us any favours, although they meant well and we were very touched by their support. They complained so much that head office actually turned it on us and blamed us for sleeping in the car, cancelling our contract for the rest of the season as a result.

So there we were, no work for the rest of the summer.

Barry went back to Rotherham while Anna and I stayed near Yarmouth because of her summer show for Duggie Chapman. I signed on the dole for the first time in my life. I hated doing that but it was a need at the time as Anna's money was not enough for the two of us and all the shows were already booked up with acts.

Our Dad used to tell us that show business was a bit of a rat race and he did his best to discourage us from going full-time. There were times like this one when his words seemed to be quite right. We wouldn't give up though.

Anna saw out her season and I had a fairly lazy time although there was a lot of golf with the various entertainers who were in Great Yarmouth for the season. Cannon and Ball, Norman Collier and Frank Carson were among the regular golfers and of course, I always ran a book on who would win, just as in the past.

Playing against Bobby Ball one day my putt stopped on the very edge of the hole. Bobby was delighted because it would have meant him winning. You are allowed to claim thirty seconds to see if it will drop into the hole so I did and I jumped up and down just once some yards away. The ball dropped into the hole. I was delighted. Bobby accused me of cheating but I had not done anything that was not in the rule book. I won the hole and the match.

Another day I played against Norman Collier, another very funny guy. His stage act included a gag in which he impersonated a chicken. He was brilliant at it and no matter how many times you saw it, you could not help but laugh out loud. On the day we were playing we got to the first green. I selected my putter, turned round and there was Norman doing his chicken impersonation while stalking his ball. It was hilarious and I could not take my putt for a while because I could not stop laughing. I still laugh about it when it comes to mind.

Haven't we lost some great comedy stars – Norman, Peter Butterworth, Norman Wisdom, Tommy Cooper, Eric Sykes – the list goes on and on. They were genuinely funny men with barely a swear word between them. Join me in a round of applause.

Even when the weather was rainy we all turned up at the golf club for a drink, a game of snooker and a chat. I have always liked a game of snooker.

I remember hearing the tale of an old chap who died at the age of 99 and had been a member of the golf club for more than eighty years, including several spells as captain. Throughout all that time he had always had a problem with the 18th hole. About two hundred members turned up on the day his ashes were to be scattered on the course. They took the urn to the 18th and tipped the urn. A gust of wind appeared from nowhere and blew his ashes off the green and out of bounds!

After a few club dates we were at last back into our pantomime season and this time we were at the New Theatre, Coventry with Tom O'Connor and Peter Butterworth once again playing Widow Twankey. Needless to say we were the Chinese policemen again in *Aladdin*.

It was great to meet up again for rehearsals and we were all set for a happy panto season but as it happens it was to be a memorable one for the wrong reason. Rehearsals went well, we had a lot of laughs and the ticket sales were great. Everything was set for a brilliant run and it did start really well. Then just before a matinee the company manager called into our dressing room to ask us if we had seen anything of Peter Butterworth. Peter had always been in his dressing room early so that he could take his time over his make-up, but there was no sign of him.

We had been out for a meal with him the night before but we had not seen him since. So the company manager went over to the hotel and asked the manager to open his room and that is where they found him. It seems that he had passed away while getting into bed, probably just a few minutes after we had left him the night before.

We soon received the dreadful news and I confess that I immediately reached for the gin bottle that I kept in my dressing room. It was the only way I was going to cope with the matinee performance which was due to start in about fifteen minutes. Of course it was a stupid thing to do as gin depresses you anyway and I was already sad enough. Most of the staff were told that Peter was not well and even his understudy did not know the truth at that stage.

That was one of the most difficult shows I have ever done. Our entrance came after Peter's opening spot as Widow Twankey and listening to the understudy doing Peter's routine was so very painful. I wish really that we had not been told either. We spent the whole show trying to be funny while fighting back the tears we wanted to shed. Between performances the whole cast were told the sad news and I have never seen so many tears not at a funeral.

Peter was the nicest gentleman anyone could meet and evidently that shrapnel had finally done its work and stopped his heart nearly forty years after hitting him. God bless you, Peter. I hope we may meet again, but not just yet, eh?

The following summer we were without a season again. The problem was that we had no manager and looked after ourselves. That was fine when things were okay but not when we had to ask for work as neither Barry nor myself liked to do that. Waiting for the phone to ring doesn't always work so while the phone did get busy for pantomime, it was very quiet, too quiet, for summer seasons.

We couldn't face doing clubs all the way through the summer so I took a job with Walls Ice Cream in Sheffield. Ever since the age of fourteen when I sold ices out of a three-wheel bicycle freezer in Clifton Park, Rotherham, I had fancied selling ice cream from a proper van.

Anyway, the deal was that Walls would lend me the van into which I put the petrol and buy all the ice cream from them. As an example I would pay 55p for a family block of ice cream and sell it for £1.25p. It worked out at about 40-50 per cent profit on everything I sold.

I soon got into the swing of it and would stock the van on Monday morning and then stock it again on Tuesday from the money I had taken on Monday afternoon and evening. I did this every day until Saturday by which time I had a fully crammed van full which was all paid for. Saturday and Sunday were the peak days of course and my chimes brought them out of their houses and lining up for ice cream.

On Sunday I really hit the jackpot. I had just started my round at about 11.30am in Rawmarsh, Rotherham. I turned a corner and there were thousands of people around the playing fields with not an ice cream van in sight. It was a hot day and the event was a national ladies football tournament, with people taking part from all over the country. I had a van full of ice cream but by 1.30pm I did not have one more thing to sell. It was fantastic and I wished I could have stocked up again and returned. I had some really good days, but never one like that again.

By the way, did you know that it is illegal to sound your chimes after 6.30pm? Not many people do, that's why you often get driven crazy by the sound of *Popeye The Sailor Man* at about 8pm. Thought I'd just mention that in case anyone else wants to have a go at selling ice cream. Live music would be better – you could always play the cornet!

I was taking home about £250 a week which wasn't bad in 1979 and certainly better than sitting at home waiting for something to happen.

There was also some better news on the work front. We had already been booked for pantomime at the Davenport Theatre in Stockport but in addition Jimmy and Brian contacted me to ask if I would like to join them on the Ken Dodd show on TV. Ken wanted to have the three little pigs tap dancing and had contacted them – the Patton Brothers – because they were well known as about the best tappers in the business for that kind of thing. Of course there were only two of them so they asked me to make up the third.

We wore dress suits and had on these big plastic pigs heads. I remember Jimmy getting claustrophobic with his plastic pig head on and starting to panic because he felt he couldn't breathe. Barry would have been the third pig because he was a better tapper than me but he had a paper shop and couldn't get away.

We also appeared in a sketch with Ken and Faith Brown. They were in bed together and Ken asked her: "Am I the first?"

Faith then looked at him with a big smile and charmingly replied: "Of course you're the first Ken… then it's John, then Jimmy, then Paul, then Brian." As she said that the camera slowly panned to show us all in the bed behind Ken.

He was very off-the-wall was Ken. He still is and very much one of the greats, a real legend and still packing theatres wherever he appears.

One day Barry and I were having a chat with Jimmy and

Brian and had the idea of working as a foursome. There had not been a comedy act with four brothers since the Marx Brothers so we got our heads together and threw lots of ideas around.

The format we came up with was also a little off-the-wall with us all having a different character. Brian was to be the straight man with Jimmy the simple one, Barry the funny, bandy one and I was to be the slightly camp one – what an actor!

What should we call the act? The Four Pattons? The Laughter Brothers? The Comedy Brothers?

I don't know who finally came up with the name we settled on but of course, it simply had to be THE CHUCKLE BROTHERS!

Chapter 8

How We Played 4-2-4

So the Chuckle Brothers were born as a four-handed act and it seemed to score with the agents and producers as we did four television shows in three months including the then-popular *Lenny and Jerry* show from the Talk of the Town near London's Leicester Square, a fantastic venue where all the major international stars appeared.

The only problem with the act was that because there were four of us we had to earn £1,000 a week which would give us £200 each and allow for the manager's 20 per cent. Yes 20 per cent. The days of managers and agents receiving 10 per cent disappeared many years ago. We were still in the 1970s and £1,000 per week was not easy to come by. We decided to persevere though because we felt we had something good. So we continued, but split for pantos and then came back together again afterwards. That's how we came to play 4-2-4!

We teamed up with John Inman again at Stockport for the pantomime but this time we were not too happy with the show. It wasn't anything to do with us or John or any of the cast but the director was one of those arty sorts who wanted everything to look pretty with lots of singing and dancing. We just did as we were told but really, anyone with any knowledge of panto will tell you that it is all about comedy and the shouting of the audience. Yes of course you have to have a few songs and some dance production numbers but if you have too many songs and dances they become toilet breaks for the kids. The mums and dads don't relax because the kids are restless and it just doesn't work properly.

When we are able we always go really heavy on comedy in pantomimes because if people go home laughing you know they have enjoyed it. You can't laugh unless you have enjoyed something. Of course you want the audience to shout but even that can go wrong. Barry and I have seen pantos in which there is too much shouting. Almost everyone that comes on the stage tells the audience to shout something every time they walk on. It's too much. You only need one character, or in our case, a pair of characters, to do that. Also, you want the traditional "He's behind you!" but not every few minutes.

We were not too upset when the panto run came to its close and we went back to the four-handed act, The Chuckle Brothers. We even performed on *The Good Old Days* on BBC TV. What a fantastic show that was. You can still see our performance on YouTube. I don't know how it got there but I'm not complaining. There's loads of stuff of Barry and me as well.

We really wanted a summer season and our manager was trying hard to get us one. The problem was money of course. Jerry Stevens of the *Lenny and Jerry* TV show wanted us in Southend with him but there was not the budget available for us four. Then, out of the blue, I got a phone call from our brother Brian who said: "We've got a summer season for Butlins." That was great news until he told me that the "we" was him and Jimmy. I was a bit disappointed to say the least but Brian explained that they had to look after their families.

I could not believe what he was telling me but there was nothing I could do about it.

So, Brian and Jimmy went back to being The Patton Brothers. And us? Well, perhaps it was a blessing in disguise because we went back to being a two-handed act – The Chuckle Brothers.

Our manager went back to Jerry's management and we were booked straight away for the summer season at Southend with Jerry topping the bill with the Second Generation, Alan Randall and the brilliant illusion act Emerson and Jayne with their amazing Flying Carpet routine.

Barry and I have always liked illusion acts. One of our favourites was an act we worked with in a Barnsley panto. It was called Skeleton's Alive and it totally amazed the audience and us as parts of skeletons went in all directions and the skeleton even flew over the audience. It was actually a lad on a rope but I don't think it would be allowed these days because of Health and Safety. If the guy had lost his grip he would have crashed straight into the audience and someone would surely have been hurt. Still, I never heard of it going wrong, the skeleton never crash landed and every audience that saw that act was blown away by it, us included.

We almost always make sure we have a really good illusion act in our Chuckle Brothers stage shows these days and for some time now we have had the brilliant Safire on the show, Stuart and Jayne. We like watching them, too.

At Southend we soon got down to the serious business of organising the golf for the season. Jerry, Alan, Barry and I all played and Jerry knew a family called the Benaleks who were well known in amateur golf circles. They even had their own course just off the Southend seafront and they agreed to let us play there throughout the summer without charging us a penny. It was a very generous gesture and we were delighted to accept their kindness. It was a beautiful course and if you are ever down there I would recommend you take a look and have a round if you play golf.

I mentioned Alan Randall before, nice guy and fantastically talented. He was a really good golfer too but he did take it all very seriously and to say he sometimes lost his cool would be an understatement.

Alan had his then 16-year-old son caddy for him and the funniest moment ever was when Alan miss-hit with a four iron for the fifth or sixth time that day. He was having a bit of a nightmare game. After mis-hitting he turned and hurled his club like a helicopter blade. It flew through the air and landed far out into a lake at the side of us. His son started after it as if this was quite normal and Alan stopped him and told him to leave it where it was. We walked about fifteen yards up the fairway when Alan changed his mind. He had obviously calmed down in that short time and he told his son to go and fetch the club. His son said nothing but removed his shoes and socks and waded in about thirty or forty yards to retrieve the club.

Alan Randall was a one-off. That was not the only strange but hilarious moment we shared with him on the golf course, but perhaps more of that later.

At the end of the summer season we wanted to say a special thank you to everyone at the golf club so we asked for them to arrange a meal for the four of us along with the captain, the secretary and of course, the Banalek family. It was a great afternoon with some super banter and stories. We played four matches against them and got thrashed before sitting down for our meal.

When it came to paying they would not let us pay a thing and said that it had been a pleasure to have us at the club for the summer. We had played there all summer for absolutely nothing and we wanted to show our appreciation but they would not hear of it. What great people they are, really generous and just a pleasure to know.

I used to go clubbing sometimes with Second Generation after the show and I'm sure their PR man that summer was a young guy named Simon Cowell. I could be wrong, but we did have some fun. If you are reading this Simon, was it you?

I behaved myself when we went clubbing even though it was an odd situation as my then wife, Anna, was in Argentina, dancing with a touring circus so I was more or less on my own. I got up early most mornings to go and play golf so I never stayed out too late when we went clubbing.

In the autumn of 1980 Anna returned from Argentina and I managed to get her into the same pantomime as us, which was great. We were topping the bill for the first time in panto and were doing *Puss in Boots* at the Adam Smith theatre in Kirkcaldy, Fife. I love Scotland and Kirkcaldy was great because it is the home of Raith Rovers Football Club as well as being the home of one of my favourite visitor attractions – the Haig Scotch Whisky distillery!

Anna and I had bought an old caravan which we parked outside the stage door of the theatre, very handy for work but freezing cold up there, with temperatures regularly dropping several degrees below. One night it actually registered twenty degrees below and we had the gas ring on all night!

We bought a dog before we went up to Kirkcaldy. He was a kind of mongrel with some Labrador in him. You never hear the word mongrel anymore. People cross breed dogs and give them a fancy name as if they are a new species. So, we had this "mongrelab" who was really black and started growing into the Hound of the Chucklevilles! He didn't get on with other dogs whatsoever but he was a really good guard dog and nobody bothered us in our caravan.

One day the heavens opened and within a short space of time we were in a couple of feet of snow. The show was called off that day and since other members of the cast regularly popped round to our caravan for a cup of tea, about six of them turned up and we had an unexpected party. We all went round the front of the theatre and started snow fights. Then I had this idea of building a massive snowman right there in front of the venue.

By the time we had built it, the idea had changed a little and what we actually made was a massive Puss in Boots sitting on a throne. If I say so myself, it was a work of art. Lots of people commented on how good it was and even the local press came down and took pictures. It was about ten feet tall and took a fortnight to melt. It turned out to be a brilliant bit of publicity for the pantomime and helped make up for the loss of that day's performance. I wish we'd had mobile phones in those days as nobody had a camera at the time and we couldn't photograph it ourselves. It was good, though.

While we were between performances one day we received a phone call to the venue from a guy who was putting the summer show into Lowestoft. Barry went to the office at the front of the theatre and came back with a big smile on his face. There and then our summer season had been booked and we were going to do a summer season with Don Maclean. We were not only delighted but relieved, as good summer seasons are often difficult to get.

We learned that Don had asked for us especially so that we could do the flying act with him again, as we had done in panto. It was a good twelve-week season, with Don doing six weeks and Leslie Crowther topping the bill for the other six weeks. There was another young man doing his first summer show and we were asked if we would mind sharing a dressing room with him. That's how we met Bobby Davro for the first time.

Bobby and I became very good friends that summer, knocking about everywhere together. We got into CB radios in our cars and he had the handle "Comedian" and mine was "Yorkshireman". At least mine was accurate!

Once again there were some happy memories from that show and that summer season. I recall Bobby buying an air rifle and we spent some time shooting things through the dressing room window. Nothing live, you understand, just things that wouldn't get hurt.

We played golf of course. Usually it was at Gorleston Golf Club, a nice course.

Bobby was a really good golfer and probably could have turned pro if he had not been an entertainer. His brother was a professional and he was brought up around Wentworth Golf Course so it was little wonder that Bobby could really play well.

If Bob had a fault it was that he didn't take it seriously enough. He just loved to play the game for its own sake and had no real ambitions to be a golf star. Perhaps that is the right attitude but it used to be frustrating to see him hit a really long and accurate drive and put himself in a fantastic position and then not trying too hard to get a really low score. We had some great games though.

There were the usual parties through the summer as well and they were fun. That is the whole essence of summer seasons or any other season. We work hard on stage and in our preparations and rehearsals, so when we have the chance we do let our hair down a bit. I suppose to some people it might seem that we just walk on stage, do our bit and then laze around the rest of the time while they are working. It's not quite like that. In fact we are working when they are relaxing to provide the entertainment that helps them relax – hopefully!

I'll never forget one evening the stage manager doing a very stupid thing which was intended to be a joke but turned out not to be very funny. I urged him not to do it and I washed my hands of the whole thing when he insisted on going ahead.

Bobby Davro had a phobia of spiders back then. I had seen him with them at his pad in Great Yarmouth and knew he could be terrified at even a little one in his wash basin. What the stage manager did was put quite a large spider in a matchbox and leave it on Bobby's place in our dressing room.

When Bobby opened the box he let out an almighty scream and dropped it on the floor, at the same time flinging himself backwards to get away from it and thumping his back on the wall. It was frightening to see but even more frightening for Bobby of course. Even worse he blamed me as I was the one who knew of his phobia. I pleaded with him and told him that I would never do such a thing to a mate but I don't think he ever really believed me.

To this day he probably still thinks I was involved but I wasn't. If you are reading this Bobby – IT WASN'T ME!

Things were going quite well for us but we were still trying very hard to become recognised as a front-line comedy act, which was not easy of course. One night though we appeared in a charity event in Great Yarmouth and though I don't like to say it myself, we stormed them. During our act Bobby Ball walked in with his then manager Laurie Mansfield who is a good friend of mine now. All Laurie could say afterwards was that he thought we were too old-fashioned and "Wouldn't go very far". To this day we still see a brick wall in front of us with the words "old-fashioned". Now let me ask you, what does that actually mean?

Does it mean that it is wrong to get lots of belly laughs rather than loads of whoops? Anyone who comes to see us live goes away having had a really good laugh whether it is our own Chuckle Brothers show, pantomime or some other show in which we are appearing. We always play for big laughs, nothing too clever or needing too much deep thought from the audience. We go for pure comedy and if that's old-fashioned then I think we need to retire. Still, if the laughs keep coming – and they do – we might just go on a little or a lot longer. Old-fashioned indeed!

There, that's my latest bit of grumpy old man out of the way – back to the story.

In the autumn of 1981 I had a big decision to make and had to pluck up the courage to see it through. I had to tell my wife, Anna, what I had been feeling for a good few years of our marriage. I felt it was also unfair to her as I was no longer 'in love' with her. Don't get me wrong, I still had love for her but it was no longer the deep love that should be there between husband and wife. I wouldn't see anything bad happen to her but it was not enough to continue our marriage.

Anna and I were still relatively young and had many good years in us. She was only 28 and I was 34 so we both still had a future. It surprised me somewhat that she had not seen this coming and that she did not really feel the same way. She was upset of course and that upset me as well as I didn't want to hurt her. She didn't deserve that. It was just one of those things and better to sort it out then than possibly start to resent each other as we got older.

Anyway, we separated and I went back to my Mum's house. She was none too pleased, I can tell you. In Mum's day you wed for life not just for Christmas and she made quite sure I knew her opinion. I felt pretty wretched as you might imagine. Life was not such a chuckle right then.

Anyway, what was done was done. Anna saw a solicitor, a lady, who asked her for reasons for the divorce.

"Did he hit you?" the solicitor asked.

"No, never," said Anna.

"Did he go out with his mates and leave you at home?" the solicitor asked.

"No, never," said Anna.

"Did he have affairs while he was with you?" the lady solicitor asked again.

"No," Anna replied.

"What's his phone number, I'd like to go out with him," said the solicitor.

The only way to get a quick divorce in those days was for there to be a good reason. We really didn't have one but I agreed to the solicitor putting down something totally fictitious for the matter to be resolved and the pain to be ended as quickly as possible. I gave Anna everything we had, which was perhaps not a lot but it did include the furniture and so on. It was a fresh start for both of us.

Pantomime that year was a magic one for me at the Swansea Grand Theatre as it was a chance to appear with Harry H. Corbett of *Steptoe and Son* fame. He was actually not well during the season and often looked quite spaced out. What none of us knew was that he had terminal cancer and three weeks after the panto he passed away. Reflecting on that, what a real pro that man was. It never showed in his performance.

I wish we had known because there was so much we could

have talked about and asked him. He was a very nice guy, a genuine man and we had quite a few chats, but not enough. You don't get many chances to meet and work and get to know people like that and when you think you might have the chance again some day, you don't always take full advantage of the time you have with them.

It was the same with Arthur Askey and Dickie Henderson back in the 1974-75 panto season. We could have learned so much from those great pros but you never think that this is your last chance to talk to them.

I don't want to get morbid but I always try to make time for guys in our business who want to learn but it's amazing how few ask questions today. How do people learn about a business if they don't ask? We always did, we constantly wanted to improve and to learn from the experience of those who were ahead of us in years. It's worrying sometimes.

Anyway, every night after the show I would make my way to the night club around the corner from the theatre and usually stayed until the music stopped at two in the morning. They played the same number every time to end the night, *Start spreading the news, I'm leaving today.* How about that for a hint! I made lots of new friends every evening at the club but we had better not go into that. I was now single, you understand. Maybe that will be in the next book!

I was driving a Nissan Bluebird in those days and one time on my way to the theatre for a matinee as I drove along the seafront a car came straight out of a side road near to the rugby and cricket ground and hit my front end, knocking me almost into a bollard. I jumped out of the car to see my nearside wing and wheel totally crushed in and it was pretty clear that my car was going nowhere.

The car that hit me was a big Mercedes Benz and the driver

Freddie "I'm Telling You Now".

Crackerjack tour 1984.

*Pantomime in
1984 at Cardiff
New Theatre
starring our good
mate Stu Frances
and Ruth Madoc.*

Barry in the rehearsal rooms for ChuckleHounds 1985.

Summer review show at Butlins Pwllheli North Wales in 1985.

Paul in his first Cabriolet. Golf, of course.

Paul before putting on weight.

Fish supper.

ChuckleHounds in Great Yarmouth 1986. We were appearing in the Circus there.

Paul and Barry, summer season Hippodrome Circus, Great Yarmouth. We were the run-in clowns and the ChuckleHounds also made an appearance.

Paul's wedding day 1986.

Paul's 40th birthday party.

With Mick Miller and Linda Nolan in 1987.

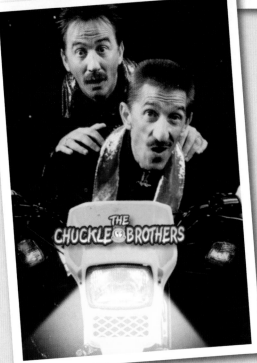

*Summer season
Weymouth in a scene
from Grease.*

Smile please.

Learning a script for ChuckleVision. Behind us is the area for a rhinoceros.

Paul and Sue at a charity event in Bradford.

*Did anyone see the film
'Weekend at Bernies?'*

Paul on holiday with his wife Sue and two youngest kids.

Family picture. Paul, Barry, Colin and Sheila
(both passed away and very dearly missed),
Brian and Jimmy.

Our family at a wedding.

Barry in mediaeval gear. ChuckleVision.

Same episode. Barry and Paul in the stocks. It was a very cold and wet day in the forest.

My 50th birthday cake given by the crew on ChuckleVision whilst filming.

Barry and Paul with Robert Duncan in panto in 1997.

Us in the dressing room at Birmingham Hippodrome.

*Barry the chicken.
ChuckleVision episode,
possibly around 2001.*

*Cover of the brochure
for 'Raiders of the
Lost Bark' tour 2002.*

A signing session at our beloved Rotherham United.

Paul with Anthony Costa of Blue.

With Crissy Rock.

*Red Nose Day
with David
Walliams who we
admire greatly.*

Panto in Darlington Christmas 2013.

and his mate got out, smelling very strongly of drink. He was full of apologies and begged me not to involve the police as they had just come from a charity event. He said he would pay for all damages and he gave me his card and details. Like an idiot I agreed. It was a huge mistake.

When I phoned him he refused to speak to me except on one occasion when he said his insurance was dealing with it. So, I was without a car for three months and all for driving along minding my own business and then trying to be a nice guy and sympathetic towards a drink driver. Trying to be reasonable doesn't always work in your favour and I was a real idiot on that occasion. You try not to let things like that sour you though and I have never stopped trying to be reasonable in difficult circumstances.

I ended up that panto season staying in an area called Treboath in Swansea at the house of a girlfriend's parents. She and I had a relationship that lasted a couple of years, not all the time in Swansea though. I probably spent about six months there. I like Swansea.

In the spring of 1982 after the dust had settled on the panto season we had a phone call from an agent in the North East of England who knew our act and asked if we would like to do an Easter theatre tour with his main act, Ward Allen, who was a ventriloquist with a great puppet called Roger the Dog.

Of course we jumped at the chance as theatres were always our favourite and we felt we were at our best on a theatre stage rather than doing clubs. Ward Allen did variety shows and also children's shows and when we were told that this was to be a children's show we nearly hesitated for a moment as we had never done an actual children's show before, family shows yes, but a children's show was something new.

We told him that we had not done a children's show before

119

but he was quite keen to go ahead and said that since we had done plenty of pantomimes we were at least halfway there. All he wanted was for us to compère the show and do some of the silly stuff we did in our pantomime routines.

That seemed to make it a lot easier and overcame any concerns we might have had. The thought of three weeks of touring during the school Easter holidays was pretty good as well, so we agreed and looked forward to it.

It is amazing how things work out in life. If we had not accepted that gig we would not be where we are today as the Chuckle Brothers with our own touring show and, of course, *ChuckleVision*.

One of the tour dates was Ashton-under-Lyne in Manchester and for the matinee performance we looked out and found that there were only about 28 people in the audience. How are you supposed to work to just 28 people in a reasonably sized theatre? How could you get any atmosphere going? We were not looking forward to it as we waited for the curtain to go up but we always remembered our Dad's words about giving the audience your best no matter what. So when the show started we went on stage really fired up and determined to give them as good a show as we could.

If I remember rightly there were about twelve mothers and sixteen kids in that audience and no sooner did we appear than Barry went down and sat with them in the stalls. I told him to get back on the stage straight away but he just folded his arms and said: "No way, it's a lot better down here than it is up there."

That did it and from then on whatever we did the audience loved. That tiny group was eating out of our hands and the show went really well. We said a silent thanks to our Dad after that performance. He was right of course and that is something I would always try to pass on – if you have a small audience give them everything you've got. It is not their fault that nobody else turned up and they need to feel appreciated, so go for it. Also you never know who from the business is watching you – as we discovered.

The very next day after that matinee we had a phone call from a man with a very posh voice. I was impressed even before he actually told us what he was phoning us about.

"My name's Peter Ridsdale-Scott from the BBC," he said.

Obviously we thought it was a mate putting on an accent and trying to wind us up so we laughed and said: "Yeah, yeah, who is it really?"

"I am Peter Ridsdale-Scott from the BBC in Manchester. I am the producer of Ward Allen's television show, *Roger the Dog* on Children's BBC and I was watching your show yesterday with my director Martin Hughes."

We couldn't believe it. Of all the shows to see it had to be one in which there were only 28 people in the audience.

"That's what we liked about you," he said when I mentioned that it was such a small audience. "The ability you showed in working to so few people and yet make them laugh was exactly what we were looking for. In a television studio that's all you have to work to, a camera crew, lighting people and so on, a small group of people. Would you like to come over to Manchester for lunch and a chat as we would like to use you in the next series of *Roger the Dog*?"

We agreed immediately of course and were walking on cloud nine. It is not every day that you get asked to have lunch with the BBC to discuss going into one of their shows. We were totally elated. We had appeared on television before, of course, but never for a series. Was this to be the start of something special for us?

We arrived at the Piccadilly Hotel in Manchester for lunch with Peter and Martin and got on really well, especially with Martin. By the time lunch was finished the deal was laid out for us and of course, we accepted. They would then take us to the costume department on Oxford Road where the old BBC Manchester headquarters used to be.

Costumes? What costumes, we wondered. When we got to Oxford Road we soon found out.

I don't know how many of you remember the show *It's a Knockout* but it was hugely popular all over Europe in the 1970s. For those who don't know what I am talking about, *It's a Knockout* was a fun competition in which people dressed up in all sorts of crazy costumes and had to race over obstacle courses and the suchlike, often getting soaked in the process. It was great fun for those taking part and even more fun for those of us watching. It ran for quite a few years and was one of the highlights of each summer. The costumes got bigger and better as the years went by and that was what went through our minds when we saw the costumes we were to wear for the television series.

Peter and Martin introduced us to two great dog costumes. There was a rather large, brown and white Bassett Hound costume which was for Barry and for me there was a massive grey Labrador costume. They were brilliant and hilarious costumes but made us immediately wonder what we were supposed to do in them.

They wanted us to be Roger the Dog's staff. Roger the Dog is starting to sound like some kind of London gang leader, or am I losing my marbles?!

Anyway, they wanted us to just fetch and carry for Roger. We said that we felt that that was a waste of their potential and said so. Peter and Martin asked what we meant so we explained that our strength was visual humour and we felt that the two 'dogs' were crying out to be used in that manner.

To their credit they asked us to go away and think about it for a week and come up with some ideas of what we had in mind. We did exactly that and returned the following Wednesday to Oxford Road armed with about thirty short sketches. Many of them were Laurel and Hardy and other silent movie comedy star gags which we knew we could adapt.

Peter and Martin loved them and decided to put a ChuckleHounds section in the show each week. We named the dogs that for obvious reasons. If you weren't going to see our faces you would at least see our name.

When the shows were edited our little bits went in every few minutes so we appeared in five slots every show. After those shows had been broadcast the BBC did a survey. I don't know if they still do it but the BBC used to send someone to travel around the country asking kids in different areas what they thought of the BBC shows, if they liked them, what they liked best and so on. The result for our show was that 83 per cent of children in the UK thought that the ChuckleHounds was the best part of the show. That was brilliant news for us of course but not so good for Ward Allen and Roger the Dog.

Chapter 9

Barking Mad as ChuckleHounds

We were delighted with the way things were going and not being seen as ourselves did not pose a problem for us. It got better still when Martin phoned and told us we were being offered our own show but had to come up with a pilot for the powers-that-be to get the go-ahead. Martin was a super guy with some fabulous ideas of his own and between us we came up with something that we thought might clinch the new series.

Anyway, we had been rehearsing for the pilot for about a week when Martin phoned and asked if he could come over to our house at Maltby. It was still Mum's house of course. This was a bit of a worry, especially when he said he had some news for us and would prefer to actually see us face to face. We thought that he was coming to tell us that the whole thing had fallen through and while we liked Martin we were not looking forward to his visit.

The rehearsals had been going well. Barry and I acted as compères to ourselves. We would introduce the act and when the curtains parted it was us doing some of our routines.

I think it looked better on television than it sounds here, with me trying to explain. Hopefully some of you saw it.

So, we were steeling ourselves for a big disappointment, but we need not have worried. When Martin arrived he told us over a mug of tea that he had quite a lot of the budget left over and wondered how we would feel about recording an additional special pilot of *ChuckleHounds* in a different environment. He favoured doing a Christmas special and we could not think of a better idea at that time of the year, so we went with the Christmas theme.

As we were to record this in November it fitted in perfectly with everything else and the ChuckleHounds were to have a little cottage of their own. Martin came up with a novel way of shooting it. The studio was to be lit extremely light with all lights burning brightly. Then he would hang a window frame and / or door frame with a door on wires which could not be seen on camera because of the brightness of the lights. It looked really good and was quite cheap on set building of course. It was very hot to say the least, especially when you are inside quite a heavy dog costume. Try it yourselves when you get home!

The storyline was that it was Christmas Eve and the dogs were putting up the decorations. Barry's character kept getting it wrong (according to my Labrador character) and I kept throwing him out into the door, slamming the door each time. Of course, every time the door slammed some snow would fall off the roof onto Barry.

You see, even with the ChuckleHounds I was the bad guy who treated Barry poorly. It wasn't really like that at all and never has been. You ask Barry and if he says that I am bad to him I'll bash him.

When Barry got back into the little house, which he always managed to one way or another, I always did my double-take. Eventually it was time to go to bed so we put our stockings at the end of the bed for Santa to fill. Barry had a bigger stocking than me so I threw mine away and got another one, this time bigger than Barry's. Barry looked at it and then went and got another to replace his, one that was bigger still.

This went on and on until Barry came in dragging a stocking that was bigger than himself. At that point I grabbed him by the scruff of the neck, dragged him to the door and threw him out. Once again the door slammed and down came the snow on his head.

The next scene was me snoring in bed and some jingle bells started to sound outside. I sat up and heard a knock at the door. I leaped out of bed and dashed to let Father Christmas in. Of course I didn't recognise that it was little ChuckleHound wearing a white beard and pretending to be Santa until his beard fell off. I gave him a big smack on the nose, something which you could do in 1984 without anyone complaining.

The show ended with us playing games on Christmas morning, like you do. Barry opened a box with 'Pin the Tail on the Donkey' on the cover. Barry placed the donkey on the door, blindfolded me and handed me the tail. He spun me round a couple of times and then edged me towards the donkey to pin the tail on it. As I reached the door he opened it and I walked out into the snow. Barry slammed the door shut and the snow fell on me. I turned back towards the door and angrily banged on it to get in – a bit like Fred Flintstone. That is where it ended.

We wrote the whole thing between us in a couple of hours

in Mum's lounge and to be honest we were quite chuffed with it. Now it was up to the people who made the decisions at the BBC.

The week after recording both pilots we immediately started pantomime again. We were back in South Wales but this time in Cardiff with Stu Francis, who became a very close friend of ours. The show was *Robin Hood* which used to be called *Babes in the Wood* but with modern-day political correctness you can't call it that any more.

I ask you, is there any wonder that we all become grumpy old men when you start to think about all the nonsense we have to put up with under the name of political correctness? I am totally against discrimination of any sort but sometimes I think that things have gone so far the wrong way that those who might be accused (usually wrongly) of discrimination are actually the ones who are discriminated against themselves. It is a confusing and crazy world in which the smaller issues are made big and the bigger issues are swept aside altogether.

Anyway, the 'Babes' panto was always one of our favourites as it was brilliant for a double act. We played the two robbers who had to kidnap the Squire's two children and take them to the woods to do away with them.

It might seem that the robbers were really evil villains but in fact they were a couple of bungling idiots, a great part for us to play.

Don't start on the typecasting jokes again!!

Thinking about it, perhaps the story line is a bit odd but of course, the Babes don't get killed and nobody really believes that they will. The two comedy bad guys couldn't open a tin of rice pudding between them, let alone do something more serious. Still, if the Babes feature these days they usually just get lost in the forest and are not in danger of anything more horrible than bumping into villainous people who you know are losers from the start.

Panto is a funny form of entertainment really. The villains consider they have done their job properly if the kids hate them, the good guys are often girls and the Dame is a bloke.

It could only happen in a real pantomime and still be family entertainment. We should be proud of our British panto heritage even if some people from other countries think we are a little eccentric, especially Australians – who gave us Dame Edna Everage!

As well as Stu Francis, Ruth Madoc was also in the Cardiff panto. Barry and I were the robbers, as I previously said. We were to take the Babes but we were such hopeless characters that the Babes would escape with the help of the Good Fairy while we were arguing about who was going to do the deed, as neither of us wanted to.

Ruth was in *Hi-de-Hi* at the time and very popular. She was a really good actress too. Of course, you can't call female actors actresses any more. You have to just call them actors. What difference does it make – a manager, a manageress, an usher, an usherette, an actor, an actress? All those words do is tell you what gender they are, is that such a crime? Before long we shall have to call those four-legged creatures from which we get milk some fancy title like 'herd associates'.

I'm going grumpy again. I can't help it, sometimes I hear things which make life seem like watching Rotherham United lose at home.

There was a scene in that show which was rather heavy for a pantomime but pretty good all the same. Robin Hood had all his Merrie Men – including Stu, Barry and me – around a camp fire (that's a fire in the middle of the camp – stop making up your own jokes!). Robin had gathered us together to tell us of his plans against the evil Sheriff of Nottingham. The scenery was very modernistic as the writer wanted to take it into the West End after the show finished its run in Cardiff. Stu, Barry and I were not to go with it but the scenery would be the same of course.

The scene had two big black trees which were great props. You could climb either of them and the one we sat on was on rails because it was so heavy and during the latter part of the scene the three of us would get off the tree and gather closer to Robin to hear the rest of his plans. As we did so, the lighting would change to something rather more moody and the tree we had been sitting on would be slowly pulled off the stage.

On the opening night Stu, Barry and I decided that it would be better if we stayed on the tree as it was being pulled off. We were booked to be funny and we thought that would get a good laugh. We did and as the tree moved we did double-takes and waved our arms about a bit. The audience screamed with laughter and we were really pleased with the result. Ruth was not so pleased and had a go at us. We reminded her that we were supposed to be doing pantomime, not some Shakespearian drama, but I don't think she saw it from our point of view. The next day the tree had gone, never to be seen again.

We really enjoyed doing that panto and had some great laughs with Stu both on and off the stage. I remember one Saturday morning when we had a half past ten show to do, a real killer for performers. Barry, Stu and I were doing a gag together and we had been out the night before to an Italian restaurant.

I have mentioned that Barry likes plain cooking so you won't find him too involved with garlic and spices. He actually had an ordinary steak in the Italian restaurant. Stu and I were completely the opposite and couldn't get enough of all those exotic flavours.

Anyway, there we were on stage with Stu and I reeking of garlic and Baz doing his best to stand away from us. Eventually we cornered him and breathed all over him. It was a great laugh at the time but thinking back it was probably a bit silly and a bit schoolboy, but we did laugh and we often had a laugh during that panto run. There was more than once that we dried on stage, with tears running down our faces. You might think that was unprofessional but we always engaged the audience in our fun and they loved it.

There was a superb entrance for the Sheriff in that panto. The stage went into darkness and the music *O Fortuna* from *Carmina Burana* – a piece often used in horror movies – pounded out.

There, that's impressed you, hasn't it? You didn't think I would know what that music is called! I even know that it was written by Carl Orff. You thought I didn't know anything beyond The Beatles or *Let's Twist Again*!

Anyway, the stage was in darkness, the *Old Spice* or *Omen* music was pounding out and the stage smoke was making the whole place really eerie. A huge drawbridge, the full height of the stage, slowly dropped towards the audience and a very tall guy who looked about 7ft tall – he wasn't but he looked it – made his regal but villainous entrance.

It was a brilliant moment but we felt that we had to do something with it on the last night, that is tradition and the comedians are allowed to have a little licence on the very last performance. So, imagine the full works, the darkness, the music, the drawbridge and the stage smoke. As the lighting changed Barry and I stepped out holding fish and chips and saying: "It's a bit steamy in the chippy tonight."

The place just erupted and we wished we had been able to do that gag all through the panto season. Anything that has such a scary build-up is ready-made for a comedy punchline. It is the unexpected that often makes people laugh.

Our Dad told us of a gag he used to do. He had a very glamorous female singer, dressed to the nines with a beautiful sparkly dress. She would stand there singing and both looking and sounding fantastic. Suddenly, for no particular reason, a custard pie would come from behind her, usually through the curtain, and splat her in the face. The audience never saw it coming and it brought the house down every single time. It is called a shock laugh and rarely fails.

So, where were we? Oh yes, I'm getting ahead of myself. When we were rehearsing for the Cardiff panto a telephone call came in from Martin Hughes to tell us the latest news about the pilot shows. He didn't sound very upbeat and once again we thought we had got so near yet so far.

Martin quietly explained that he had managed to complete the editing of the *ChuckleHounds* pilots and sent it down the line to the powers-that-be in London. They had sat down to watch it at 11.30 in the morning, not the best of times to be asked to laugh. Martin spun the story out a bit and we waited for the punchline so that we could shrug off our disappointment and get back to panto rehearsals.

Martin told us the rest. They had sat down at 11.30 to watch it and by 11.45 they were on the phone to the publishers of *Radio Times* to tell them to change the Christmas schedules! They were going to put *ChuckleHounds Christmas* on screen at 11.50am on Christmas Eve, a brilliant spot for the show.

We were thrilled to bits of course and it got even better the next day because Martin phoned us again to say that he had been contacted once more by the people in London and had been told that they wanted a series of eleven *ChuckleHounds* shows. They also told him that they had tried to see how it was done. They thought it must be animation of some sort or perhaps puppets. Then they realised that it was actually people in the costumes. Martin told them that it was us, the Chuckle Brothers, who were the guys inside the costumes and that he had to finish editing it but he did indeed have a pilot already made.

Martin finished the editing and sent it down to London. Two days later he phoned us again to tell us that they loved the show, thought we were fabulous but also thought that they would like us to do a series as ourselves rather than as the Hounds.

Can you imagine how we felt about that! It was incredible news. After a century of being on stage and in clubs we were on the verge of being an overnight success.

We didn't get carried away. We had already experienced too many disappointments in life to trust that it was all going to go smoothly from now on. We couldn't help our excitement though. This was what we had hoped might happen one day. We started to think of the title of the show, perhaps Chuckle Television. Then another phone call came from Martin.

BBC Worldwide had been on to head office and stated that they would put up 85 per cent of the cost to make the *ChuckleHounds* as they could sell it all over the world. No dialogue meant that there were no language barriers and unlimited sales. This was not what we wanted to hear. It was good to know that the Hounds had been successful and to be a part of that success but we were disappointed that it was not going to be the Chuckle Brothers in their own right.

Martin understood and promised that he would do his best to make sure that we would get our own Chuckle Brothers show one day but money held all the cards and the BBC would do anything to save money, hence their taking the *ChuckleHounds* option when financial support was offered.

It is strange the way people think sometimes. For instance, the BBC never put *ChuckleVision* into the trade fair at which representatives from broadcasting services all over the world come to see and buy the shows that the people of their countries might like. When you consider how many countries speak English and would probably have loved *ChuckleVision*, it seems really strange to us that the BBC never, never gave the people outside Britain the chance to see the show. It would have recouped a lot of money for the BBC too, so not making any attempt to sell the show does seem very short-sighted.

During the panto at Cardiff Stu Francis introduced us to his manager. He took us on and became our manager too. Straight away we were signed to do Stu's tour of *Crackerjack!*

Yes, I heard you but there are no pencils for those who remember. I didn't realise you were that old!

The show toured the length and breadth of the UK from Aberdeen to Plymouth. I think we did about 65 dates that spring and we were reunited with another of my best pals, Charlie Cairoli Jnr. He had worked with his dad in the 1974 Blackpool Tower Circus but now, since the very sad death of his father, who was truly one of the great gents of the world – Charlie WAS Charlie Cairoli – Charlie Jnr was carrying on with some of the same stuff. He had a new Jimmy, the silent one, and his lovely wife Claudie was the new straight man who was previously a white-faced clown, or sometimes the ringmaster.

They did some very funny stuff in their routines and were great to have on the show. The whole show was great, actually. It went well with audiences everywhere we went and there was a great family spirit between us all in the company.

Sometimes that family spirit got stretched a bit. We did one date in a leisure centre and there was a sauna where we changed. We thought that was great and said we would go for a sauna between shows. I went straight after the finale so I was the first one in the sauna and got the best spot. I waited and waited, getting hotter and hotter and I was beginning to think that the others had changed their minds when Stu and Charlie peered through the little window to make sure I was still there. They smiled at me with thumbs up to see if it was working all right. I shouted to them to come in because it was great. They opened the door and Charlie threw a full bucket of icy cold water all over me.

Of course, they were in hysterics and I joined in after a couple of minutes once I had got my breath back. The shock would probably kill me now but after uttering a few choice words which cannot be printed here, I did join in the laugh.

It wasn't just the ChuckleHounds that were barking mad!

Chapter 10

Hounds, Big Cats and a Dead Ant

We had done a good panto which finished at the start of the year, got a new manager, did the *Crackerjack!* tour and had the possibility of our own television show still very much alive as well as the *ChuckleHounds* show being scheduled. We had a summer season too.

We were booked at Butlins Pwllheli in North Wales which was great as we have always liked Wales, both North and South. This time we were to be in the revue show which was staged in the theatre. That doesn't happen any more. Like many others in the holiday industry Butlins discovered that while people were sitting in a theatre they were not spending at the bar so the policy changed to put the live entertainment in a big bar room. That meant that the drinks, including soft drinks for the kids, crisps and basket meals, could keep going while the show was on.

Artistes prefer the proper theatre setting because you have more facilities on a theatre stage and you can include much better and bigger production numbers. For Barry and me the theatre is better because we can use the stage better for some of our visual gags. Also in a theatre you have the undivided attention of your audience too. Still, work in a bar show is better than no work at all.

So there we were in 1985 in a revue which in those days was still being staged in the theatre at Butlins. It was a good season and yes, we did manage a round of golf, well actually probably one or two rounds. Oh, all right. Yes there was a lot of golf, a lot of football and a lot of other fun and games too. The show went well and the season seemed to fly past.

It was soon October and we left Butlins with pantomime in Halifax looming up not too long afterwards.

Vince Hill was top of the bill in the panto and once again we found ourselves working with a really lovely man. We have been so lucky in our business to have worked with so many really nice people. As with all walks of life there are some really nasty pieces of work in the business as well. I have never been able to understand people who are arrogant about who they are. It doesn't matter who you are or what you do for a living, that's exactly what you are doing – working for a living just like everyone else.

The world only keeps going because of people working and it doesn't matter if you dig roads, clean windows, sell newspapers or run the Bank of England, you are still just part of the workforce. Just because you are on the telly, make records or play football for a Premiership side, that does not mean that you are a better person than the next. We should all think ourselves lucky that we are born with any talent or aptitude and perhaps humbly respect what other people can do rather than just promote ourselves.

There I go again on my high horse with just a touch of grumpy. Don't get cheeky, it was just a touch of grumpy.

Back to the panto at Halifax and as well as Vince Hill topping the bill we also had a well-known baddie, none other than Geoff Capes, a giant of a man but a real gent and a good pal. He is a lovely guy but you wouldn't mess with him unless you are sure that you are right. He is one of those who will always try to see someone else's point of view but has a great sense of justice and fair play and will defend it all the way. Just ask the security guy at an Olympic Games who refused to let Geoff into the stadium even though he was competing in the shot putt and was an internationally recognisable athlete. Geoff had forgotten his pass. Needless to say Geoff reasoned with him and the man changed his viewpoint. I'm glad he's a mate. You are a mate, aren't you Geoff!

I must tell you something about Vince as well. He won't mind me telling you this, I am sure. Although Vince is a fantastic singer with a brilliant voice he didn't actually want to be an entertainer. He wanted to be a pastry chef. The trouble was that he found he had an allergy to the flour and couldn't face trying to be creative while wearing gloves. They couldn't do anything for him in those days so he decided to take his father's advice and turn his part-time singing into a career which, of course, he did very successfully. He is still a great cook though.

The guys we got on best with during that panto run were Linda Nolan and her husband and manager Brian. Linda's dressing room adjoined ours with a connecting door and her husband Brian, who was always with her, wedged the door open with a table upon which lived a bottle and some glasses. Both Brian and myself were partial to a drop of Bells or Grants during the evening performance. He mixed his with Coca Cola and I mixed mine with still water. Barry, being teetotal, would have just Coke and Linda would wait until the show was over. It was quite a family atmosphere between us.

Unfortunately Brian passed away a few years ago and I know Linda still misses him so badly, as do most of us who knew him. Linda, Brian and Geoff all came to my wedding a couple of years after the panto.

While we were in the Halifax panto we would travel each morning to Manchester to film the *ChuckleHounds* series. We would drive at 7am for a 9am start and wrap about midday to drive back for a matinee. The evening show would finish at about 9.30pm and we would go back to the house we rented in the Yorkshire Dales and then get up again at 6.30am to do it all over again. Although we loved doing the panto and had a great time throughout the season it was quite exhausting and we were pleased when the panto ended and the filming became much easier.

Dave Cook, another very good friend of ours, came up from London for a day to watch some of the filming. Dave did all the music for the show and subsequently *ChuckleVision* as well.

The ChuckleHounds didn't speak. They made sounds from an electronic keyboard, although many people said they could understand every word we said, something which always baffled us since we didn't actually say anything at all. Dave was very clever with the sounds. He still is of course. He composed the theme tune for the hounds and the well-known *ChuckleVision-Chuckle-ChuckleVision* theme. Several years later he played lead guitar on our song video for Children In Need, *Silly you – Silly me*.

Dave also made several appearances in *ChuckleVision* as an extra and more famously was the musician in the silent *ChuckleVision* episode we did in the early 'Noughties'.

Our 1986 summer season saw us return to the wonderful

world of the circus. Peter Jay booked us for the summer at the Hippodrome, Great Yarmouth to do run-ins as ourselves but also to appear as the ChuckleHounds. We had done run-ins before at Blackpool so that was fine but we were a bit worried how the ChuckleHounds would go in a live circus performance.

It turned out to be a great success with the audiences. They loved the ChuckleHounds and the kids would queue up at the interval to have their photos taken with them. We sat on the circus ring and the kids came and sat with us for the photo. It was actually quite good fun and a delight to see that the ChuckleHounds were so popular.

We knew of Peter Jay from the 1960s as he was the drummer and leader of his own band – Peter Jay and the Jay Walkers. We used to go to the Baths Hall in Rotherham and see him play. He was always centre of the stage with two bass drums which were illuminated with coloured lights inside them. It looked great and he was quite a showman, something which reflected in his later promotions and especially the circus at Great Yarmouth which he still runs today.

I do remember how well he and the band used to go at Rotherham Baths. We were young and impressionable in those days but even so, those lit-up drums were quite brilliant. They were a great rock band and could really play, not just look good. Peter himself was a fabulous guy and has never changed. He gave us some great ideas which we used for many years afterwards.

The chicken song was one example. We put together with Peter an audience participation piece which involved the audience holding a pretend chicken in the air, sticking a pretend deckchair up their nose, flying a pretend jumbo jet and then burying all their clothes. We used this years later as a finale song sheet in pantomimes. The audiences loved it and it was great for holding a competition between one side of the auditorium and the other. It is a lot of fun so thanks for helping out with that one, Peter.

Circus life is full of lovely people. One thing they do every day, which I believe is quite unique, is that whenever they meet each other they shake hands. Sometimes they meet, shake hands and have a chat and then a couple of hours later they see each other again and go through exactly the same routine. I don't know of any other profession in which that takes place.

I had a great experience one day when the lion trainer took me to meet one of his special animals. It was a snow leopard, one of the most beautiful animals you could ever wish to meet. The lion trainer, by the way, had what was known as a mixed group of big cats but the one thing he didn't have was lions so it seemed a bit daft to call him the lion trainer but easier to describe what he did. He was very courageous because the big cats look cuddly and can be really friendly but you never know when they are going have a change of attitude!

Anyway I was taken to meet this lovely snow leopard and I was completely overwhelmed by actually being able to stroke this amazing big cat. It looked so dangerous and probably was but with the trainer there it was just like a big kitten. He could do anything with it and there was obviously a great relationship between them. I felt really privileged to be allowed to stroke the snow leopard.

I know some people will disagree but I can't help feeling that banning wild animals from circuses is perhaps a little heavy-handed. My own experience of people with animals in circuses during the seasons we worked at Blackpool and at Great Yarmouth was that you could not wish for better care for the animals, whether big cats, elephants, horses or dogs. They were like members of the family to those who worked with them, who spent hours showing them loving care. It was not just five minutes in the ring and that was it. There was much more to their relationship than that.

Remember, I saw it all from behind the scenes and I marvelled at the rapport between the animals and their trainers and keepers. Anyone who has ever owned a dog or a cat will tell you that they have a special kind of love for their animals and that is no different to what I witnessed and experienced first-hand behind the scenes in the circuses with which Barry and I performed.

One of the downsides to that season in Great Yarmouth was that I was quite ill for a week. It was caused by something stupid, though I would not want to blame the person concerned because he would never have thought that his actions would result in such consequences.

Our ChuckleHound costumes weighed a ton and I could only see through the nose, which was of course part of the head but a very top-heavy and huge head. In the ring we did things in which the smaller dog – Barry – would tease the bigger dog – me. It usually resulted in the little dog getting a smack from the bigger dog and taking a big tumble. The audiences loved it. Well, in one performance as we left the ring, waving to the audience, one of the ring boys decided it would be funny if he pushed the big dog over. I didn't know he was going to do that and it is true that the audience did laugh as I tumbled out of the ring.

What people didn't realise was that the heavy costume made it quite difficult for you to break your fall and as a result I bashed my hip on the edge of the circus ring.

It wasn't the lad's fault. He genuinely thought it would be funny and at about 18 or 19 he didn't think that it might actually hurt someone. Things like that don't enter your head when you are a teenager. He thought that the size of the costume probably meant that there was a lot of padding. Below the waist there wasn't and I really did hurt my hip.

I didn't realise just how much it hurt until the next day when I turned up at 8.30am for a game of golf with Roy Walker, Les Dennis and Barry. After about three holes I started feeling a pain in my groin but I thought I had perhaps pulled something so I didn't worry too much. It started getting more and more painful after each hole and I was also starting to run a temperature but we finished the game and then went to the Hippodrome and did our first performance of the day.

Between shows we went back to our accommodation and Barry phoned a doctor as I was clearly getting worse. I had to wrap myself in blankets even though it was a nice, warm, summer's day. When the doctor came he told me I had septicaemia and should be in hospital but it was too late and I shouldn't be moved. It did panic me a bit but he left me some antibiotics and told us to contact him again if things didn't improve.

I took two of the pills and then started to feel really sick. Within seconds I had brought them back up and was feeling really awful. I hated to do it but I asked Barry to ring the doctor again. Within a quarter of an hour the doctor was back and saw the state I was in. I was heaving almost all the time with nothing left to bring up. He gave me an intravenous injection which dropped the temperature within a couple of minutes and eased the sickness too.

The doctor came back later at about 11pm to give me a second jab. I thought that was really brilliant of him. How many doctors around today would have done that without being persuaded? I missed doing the show for a full week and that made me feel awful. The doctor came back every day for the next three days and eventually put me on tablets again. This time they started to work properly.

I hated missing the performances. We have always believed that the show must go on and we have worked with flu and all sorts of things but this one really floored me. I had never felt so ill in my life. It was the first of three times I was unfortunate enough to get septicaemia but the other times are another story for another time. The outcome on this occasion was that I could not wait to get back to work but had to patiently wait nonetheless until I had near enough recovered.

That whole showbiz thing about the show must go on is taken more seriously than you might imagine. Our Dad used to put on pantomimes and there were always a dozen or more dancers in them. They mostly made up the happy-clappy villagers but often did a couple of special dance spots during the performance. A couple of times one of the girl dancers would turn up with a broken leg or something along those lines. That did not mean that she couldn't work. If she was up to her neck in plaster and on crutches she could still take part by standing around as one of the villagers in a production number.

That might sound harsh but what it actually meant was that the show still had its full complement of people taking part in the performance and the girl kept her job as she recovered. Oh yes, in Dad's day he made sure that the show went on no matter what the problem. I often wish people were the same today but we don't always seem to have that approach to show business life any more. It seems unfortunate that most people seem to be in the business these days for what they can earn.

We were doing pantomime at the Birmingham Hippodrome a few years back and one day about seven weeks into the panto season we did a performance with only one dancer. There we were in what was probably the country's No 1 pantomime and with only one dancer. The others around us were dropping like flies. There were colds and flu, cuts, bruises and all sorts of things that meant that we could only manage one fit dancer on the stage. I can't help feeling that most of them could have been involved as villagers just standing around, although some of them were definitely intent on limping for as long as they possibly could.

You may wonder what we were doing between panto seasons and summer seasons but the truth is – not a lot really, certainly not much that is worth talking about. We used to see as much of Rotherham United as we possibly could and we still do.

The Millers have been very dear to us all our lives and we will never change, although I must confess that I have a second team who I also follow avidly and have done since I was a kid. Who? Dare I tell you? Oh all right then, since you insist. I am a die-hard Liverpool fan. I would always support Rotherham if they played each other. If? All right, when, as I am sure it is only a matter of time before the Millers reach the Premiership.

We have a great stadium these days and a big local population of supporters so all things are possible and I look forward to seeing the day when the Premiership fixtures include Rotherham United v Liverpool or perhaps one of those other teams from Manchester, can't remember their names.

That aside, Barry and I always spend time between seasons and shows thinking about new comedy and show ideas, writing scripts and so on. Apart from that I enjoy my holidays with a glass of something, some sunshine and a newspaper to read. That's me sorted.

When I was single I used to like to go holidaying abroad, sometimes taking someone with me. Then there are little things like changing your car, all the usual things that people do.

Before we started filming *ChuckleVision* in 1987 I actually bought my very first brand new car, an XR2 which was fantastic to drive and had loads of extras. It was a long way from the day when we went to that farmyard to buy our first van.

I am not as careful with money as I perhaps should be. I don't just throw it away on any old rubbish or whim but if I am going to have a new car I want it to be a good one and if I am going on holiday I want it to be a really good holiday. Cleethorpes is great but the Mediterranean just has the edge over it.

Our next pantomime was back in Darlington. We did enjoy it very much. It is a great theatre and we still go back there quite often and always have a great time. The staff are always so friendly and helpful and the audiences are just brilliant and determined to have some fun, exactly what we are there for as well.

It means a lot to us because our Dad worked there quite a lot with the Merry Magpies and Bobby Thompson. We used to go and see him there and even now when we go backstage it has hardly changed and brings back so many great memories.

Sunderland is the same and also Newcastle. Our Mum used to take us to visit our Dad at those theatres and while there have been improvements of course and a bit of painting and decorating they are all essentially the same and it means so much to us to have that link with our Mum and Dad.

So there we were back at Darlington with *Jack and the Beanstalk* and starring alongside Bernie Clifton, who became famous for riding an ostrich but has so much more to his talents than doing that crazy routine, and also alongside the lovely and talented Suzanne Dando.

Let me tell you that Bernie is another great guy to work with if you can live with his practical jokes. We had worked with him several times before and once, up in Ayr in Scotland, Barry and I were doing a routine which involved Barry eating a banana behind my back. As I looked away he would quickly peel the banana and stuff the lot into his mouth really fast and then look totally innocent when I turned round and looked at him. He would put the banana peel under his hat and chew the banana every time I looked away.

Eventually I would stop looking away and just stare at him as he struggled to keep his face straight with the rest of the banana still to be swallowed. After a while he would put his hand behind me and tap me on the shoulder. When I turned round Barry would try to swallow the rest of the banana. I turned back just in time to catch him pulling a face as he tried to swallow. Of course, I then gave him a telling off. Looking rather guilty he would take off his hat and put the banana skin into my hand, which would get another laugh because I would react to that.

We could probably have taken that routine a lot further with banana skin on the floor and lots of other possibilities but sometimes you have to keep a gag short otherwise it becomes a whole sketch rather than just a lengthy gag.

People we worked with were often amazed at how quickly Barry could peel and eat the banana. We actually had to drop this routine later because his digestive system couldn't take it any longer. Pity really because the banana routine always went well. Perhaps we should have tried it with a pineapple!

On the occasion I started to tell you about, we were doing this routine in the show at Ayr and we never thought it could go wrong. We had not taken into account the mad humour of Bernie Clifton! One evening he got a syringe and filled the banana we had at the ready with Wintergreen. Can you imagine taking a big mouthful of banana with Wintergreen in it? Obviously by the second mouthful the burning heat kicked in and Barry knew there was something wrong with the banana.

Being a real professional Barry knew the show had to carry

on so he continued with the gag and took another bite of banana. I knew nothing of this until I turned round and saw him for the first time. His face was bright red from the heat of the Wintergreen and Bernie and the crew, who were all in on what Bernie had done, were standing in the wings collapsing with laughter.

Barry carried on to the bitter end, so to speak. It might have been the end of him because who knows what Wintergreen might do to your stomach. I have always admired the fact that he would not give up on the gag, no matter what. He was prepared to bite the bullet – or banana in this case. At the end of it, though, his face was an absolute picture. He was bright red and almost steaming but part of that was that he was none too happy about the gag that had been played on him.

Bernie is one of those people you just can't get angry with for more than a few seconds. He just looks at you and smiles and your anger just evaporates. He has got away with all kinds of things through the years, he has been a brilliant entertainer. Did you know that he is also an extremely good singer and can perform even classical numbers? Did you also know that he is quite a musician and plays in the England supporters band that you often hear on television when an international is being broadcast? Yes, there's a lot more to our pal Bernie Clifton than just being a highly talented lunatic.

When we went for rehearsals for the panto Bernie started his pranks straight away. One day when we were out doing some publicity stunts to promote the panto we found ourselves in a shopping centre and he persuaded us to join him in a shop window where they were displaying a poster for the show.

We climbed into the shop window and stood there motionless like waxworks of ourselves. We were in full costume of course so it probably looked quite good to passers-by glancing or staring into the window. One lady stopped and really stared at us, leaning forward to get a really close look. Bernie suddenly leapt forward toward the window and frightened the life out of her. She fell backwards onto her backside with her shopping going all over the place.

I know we should not have found it so funny but it could not have worked better if it had been rehearsed and if it had been filmed it would certainly have been shown on *You've Been Framed* time and time again. We certainly cried with laughter and the lady also found it funny and was delighted when we gave her some free tickets for the pantomime for being such a good sport.

That was just one of Bernie Clifton's many pranks. Back at rehearsals he told the entire company that we had to play a game called Dead Ant throughout the run. He said it was a long tradition and we would simply have to do it. We immediately thought he was starting off one of his wind-ups again but he meant it and kept it going throughout the weeks of the panto season.

The game was that if you saw another member of the company anywhere at all, except during a performance, and they didn't see you, you would shout at them "Dead Ant!" and they would have to immediately lay on their back and kick their feet and hands in the air as though they were a dying ant.

Can you imagine the carnage this caused?! You daren't walk round a corner without looking first in case someone caught you. It was very embarrassing in the high street because you had to stop at every corner and peer round you like a very bad spy. We must have all looked like idiots who thought we were James Bond in disguise.

Bernie was brilliant at it, as he should have been since it was his stupid game in the first place. He would hide in doorways for what seemed like hours just to catch someone as they came down the street. It drove you completely mad but if you were caught you just did it no matter where you were or what else you were supposed to be doing. We often got some really funny looks from passers-by who thought we were having a fit or something.

However, we did get him back. It was a snowy afternoon and we saw him walking across a zebra crossing covered in slush. There was quite a group of us from the show out there together in the street and we all shouted at once: "Dead Ant!"

His face fell for a moment and he groaned "Oh, no!", but being the man he is he then grinned and went straight down on his back in the slush and started kicking his legs and waving his hands about. What the drivers who were waiting to continue thought we will never know but I am sure some of them must have gone home and told their families about seeing Bernie Clifton pretending to be a dying ant in the middle of a very wet and slushy zebra crossing!

Bernie was on his way to the theatre for a matinee so he got changed, hung up his clothes to dry and did the performance. The rules were changed after that so that nobody had to do the Dead Ant if the ground was wet. At least Bernie had stuck to his own rules and, more importantly, we had all got revenge!

We had a brilliant panto season right the way through to early February when we finally said goodbye for the time being to Darlington and returned to Rotherham. Barry, his wife and kids went to their home and I went back to Mother in Maltby. However, my life as a single man was about to change and the ChuckleHounds were about to give up a dog's life.

Chapter 11

A Dog's Life Suddenly Changed

Being single means that you can have a bit of fun without having to answer to anyone in particular, but it is not all its cracked up to be. At the end of the day you often go home to nobody and have no one to share your experiences with. Mums are great but sometimes you need someone else. That was me. I didn't especially want to be single but I didn't want to get married again just for the sake of it. There had to be someone special.

The last thing I expected was to meet someone on a blind date who would change the course of my life.

A close friend of mine came to me with a proposition from a friend of his girlfriend. How about that for instant complication! Anyway, this young lady had seen me on a BBC2 TV programme called *Fax*. The programme had included a piece about the legendary Wilson, Kepple and Betty and we had been asked to perform the Sand Dance that they did so brilliantly and was the hallmark of their act.

So, she saw us performing on television and mentioned it to her friend who was my mate's girlfriend. She told her that she vaguely knew me through her boyfriend and could fix her up with a blind date as she knew I was single. Are you still following me? Read it back to me as I am starting to get lost myself.

Neither the young lady nor myself had ever been on a blind date before but when my mate mentioned it I told him I could be free on the following Monday so long as I could see a photograph of her first to make sure that I was not being set up for a joke or that it was someone I knew straight away that I wouldn't get on with. She probably would have done the same if she had not already seen me on the telly.

So, a couple of days later he came back to me with a photo of Sue and I instantly agreed. She looked beautiful in the photo and if she turned out to be a Rotherham fan too, that would have made her perfect. Still, you can't have everything, can you?

The big day came the following Monday. I will always remember it because it was February 16th, two days after Valentine's Day. If I had been a real romantic I would have made it two days earlier but to be honest I was out at a party that evening. I have often been reminded of that. Still, I have never missed a Valentine's Day since. At least, I don't think I have....

We drove round to pick her up and I had never really believed in love at first sight until that moment. As she left the house and walked down to the car I just knew that we were entering a relationship and not just a night out.

I'm not totally unromantic and wanted to treat her really well so for that first date I took her to the pub. Well, what did you expect? The chippy would not have had the same atmosphere!

As we chatted I noticed that every ten minutes she kept disappearing. No, I had not had too much to drink, she just kept leaving us. For a moment I thought she had a bladder problem but then I realised that she was nipping out for a fag. I had given up smoking six years before but I could still remember what it was like to go without a cigarette for a while, especially if you were a little bit nervous. So I said nothing rather than make a joke which might ruin the whole evening.

It came to the time to go home and I said I would drop her off. I told her how much I had enjoyed the evening and as I said goodnight I leaned across to give her just a little peck on the cheek. She gasped and pulled back from me as if I had turned into a werewolf! I was quite shocked. I didn't realise I was so horrible! We seemed to have got on really well but now her eyes were popping out of her head as if she was totally shocked at the prospect of even a little kiss on the cheek!

I didn't make a fuss and just smiled and said goodnight and left it at that. We had a little wave and I drove off. It bothered me though, because I didn't want to offend her in any way and thought that I must have done.

We had exchanged telephone numbers during the evening so the minute I got home I just had to phone her to put my mind at rest. I was relieved when she told me that she had enjoyed our night out and I just had to ask her what had happened when I had leaned across to give her a little kiss. She told me that she would never kiss a guy on the first date. It was good to hear because I thought perhaps it was me. Somehow it was kind of old-fashioned but had a certain charm about it. We talked for about another hour and then I asked if it would be all right for me to pick her up from work the next day. She agreed so I went to bed that night really looking forward to tomorrow.

I was actually there a little early because she didn't finish work at the solicitors until half past three. I amused myself by playing my latest cassette purchase and never thought that having 'I was a male stripper in a go-go bar' pounding out might cause a frown or two. I think I got away with it and Sue didn't seem to mind. I took her home and met her two sons, Simon, who was then nine, and Nicholas, who was four. They had just come out of school.

Sue had also been married before and was now living on her own. We saw each other every day for the next two weeks until I went away on holiday to Spain. It had been booked for a while as a family break. Barry, Anne, their kids, Carrie who was then twelve, and Barry Jnr who was nine, also went as well as myself and our Mum. It was a special treat for Mum. She had never been abroad before in her life so going to a villa in Spain was a bit special and she used to love going to pick oranges from the grove at the back of the villa and then squeezing them for our breakfast orange juice.

Even while I was in Spain I still spoke to Sue every day and I could not wait to see her again. She seemed a bit quiet when I got back, although we were spending a lot of time together and she seemed happy about that. Eventually I got it out of her that she had stopped smoking because she knew I didn't like it and of course, she was struggling with it.

After about five weeks I moved in with her and all seemed to be going well. I was really happy.

About a fortnight later we were sitting watching TV one evening and I could see that she was craving for a cigarette. She was quiet and nervy. I told her to go to the shop and buy forty cigarettes, twenty for her and twenty for me. She didn't want to at first but I told her that I couldn't see her going through all her trauma. I had fallen in love with a different person and I wanted that person back even if it meant smoking again myself. It worked. Straight after lighting up she was back to her old self.

It seemed the right thing to do at the time but many years later I was to regret starting smoking again. I gave it up again as it did my health no favours and I would urge anyone who can give it up to do so and anyone who has never smoked, don't try it. Going back to smoking was pretty stupid of me and some health issues came as a result. Fortunately I stopped again in time.

I introduced Sue to my nephew Mick, my sister Sheila's son. We went out for a meal together a few times with Mick and his then girlfriend Dawn. She is his wife now, by the way. We knocked about quite a bit together and even went on holiday to Rhodes in April of that year. We were having a great time and the last thing I wanted to think about was work but I thought I had better phone home to Barry to see if there was anything happening for us.

"Hello Baz, weather's great here, what's it like in Rotherham?" I enquired.

"The sun's just come out," he told me.

I thought that was a bit unusual in Rotherham in April but then he told me what he meant. Moments before I phoned he had had another phone call from Martin Hughes. The news was that we had been offered our own television series as ourselves.

Martin had told Barry that they wanted us to do 26 episodes to go out on Saturday mornings before the *Going Live* show. Martin had told them that 13 episodes ought to be the limit because we might not be able to write enough material to go much further than that.

Yes, you are right, it was the start of *ChuckleVision* and we were not limited to 13 episodes. *ChuckleVision* ran for more than a quarter of a century and we recorded hundreds of shows. There are still some in the can now.

You can imagine that there were some celebrations after hearing that news from Barry. The thought that we were going to have our own Chuckle Brothers television show on BBC1 was just fantastic, a bit like winning the FA Cup. It didn't sink in for a while.

We carried on with our holiday and had a terrific time. There was one moment of awkwardness when I was getting a little amorous towards Sue and the door suddenly opened and Mick and Dawn came in. They instantly turned round rather red-faced and marched out again. Sue jumped up and hid in the wardrobe. It took me ages to coax her out because she was so embarrassed. I thought I was going to have to have meals sent in to her!

We finally went home from our holiday and the excitement about *ChuckleVision* continued. We were booked back with Peter Jay again that summer but this time we were going to return to Blackpool where he was also putting on the circus. It had been thirteen years since we first appeared there and it was good to be back. Sue packed in her job and joined me but still wanted to have a job so she found one in a local solicitors' office which worked out perfectly. Simon and Nick went to school in Blackpool and everyone was happy with their lot in life.

As for Barry and me, well, we were busy of course with circus shows near enough every day and filming for *ChuckleVision* as well, a bit like we had filmed *ChuckleHounds* while in panto. We had the best of both worlds at last.

Chapter 12

ChuckleVision Becomes a Big Hit

We were a bit nervous at the start of filming *ChuckleVision* but once we got into it the nerves soon went. We need not have worried as *ChuckleVision* became a big hit – I used to hit Barry and Barry used to hit me!

No, not really, it was a huge success I am delighted to say. We didn't know that at the time though, so the nerves were jangling a bit. It is the same when you are going on stage. A lot of experienced entertainers will tell you that the worst moment is just before you step out. I know some of them who are sick before they go on and they have been doing shows for years.

We have never been that bad but you can't help being a little apprehensive when you are about to do something new. *ChuckleHounds* had worked well and there was no reason to believe that the same would not happen with *ChuckleVision* but you never know. It is wrong to be over-confident because then things can really go wrong.

Anyway, just as it all changes and your nerves settle once the show starts, it is the same with filming. Once you are on the set you forget about any nerves and it all starts to take shape. Our experience with *ChuckleHounds* proved to be really useful because we worked with a crew of the same sort of size.

The basic plot for each show was that Barry and I found ourselves taking a job or getting involved in some other task or adventure, usually engaged by a character who became known as "No Slacking". He was of course our brother Jimmy. His "No slacking" catchphrase is still heard in many workplaces today. Our other brother Brian was also often in the cast.

We often have our catchphrases shouted at us when we are out shopping or stopping at a motorway services. It is not at all unusual to hear someone shout "No slacking" or Brian's "Geroutofit!" We also get "To Me… To You…" and also "It isn't!" "It is!" "It isn't!" "It is!" "Is it?"

In *ChuckleVision* we were the bane of Jimmy's life because he was the one who 'trusted' us to do a job properly, something which rarely happened. Of course, in real life it is not like that, is it Jimmy? Jimmy…? The adventures were a lot of fun and sometimes slightly weird but we never ever strayed from family viewing and we never did a thing that could teach youngsters the wrong approach. For instance, you never saw us plug in an electrical appliance or anything like that. We were always very careful not to set a bad example.

There was another character who featured regularly but was never ever really seen. He was "Dan the Van". Viewers often heard about him and knew we were working for him but they never saw him, except once. In one episode we had to get Dan to a meeting and he was seen on screen. He was covered in bandages and wore sunglasses so you still couldn't see him. Who was he? He was our version of *Top Gear*'s Stig, so we couldn't possibly tell you.

One of the favourite things about *ChuckleVision* was our regular mode of transport which was one of those quadricycles you often see at holiday camps. It became known as The Chucklemobile – Chuckle 1 – and had a bright red and white roof. We loved it but it was hard work to pedal. On screen you saw Barry doing all the pedalling with me with my feet up. I only pedalled twice in all the times it was featured, once when we were safari park keepers and were pedalling away to escape a lion on the loose and the other time was when we were a couple of gardeners and were making our escape after wrecking a lady's much-loved garden. In reality I did my fair share of pedalling – honestly!

In *ChuckleVision* we carried on our usual style. I was always the dominant of the two characters and took most of the decisions, although mostly it was due to my mistakes that we ended up wrecking a job or getting into some other trouble. Of course I always blamed Barry but usually by the end of each show it came out that Barry was more often in the right than me. We used to spend a lot of time running away from people at the end of each show so we had to be fit. I used to read bigger newspapers to keep my strength up and Barry used to lift bigger tea mugs!

With *ChuckleVision* we did a lot of location work as well as our studio shoots and of course we often had quite a few extras. You can't call them "extras" any more. Just as you cannot call actresses "actresses" any more, you have to call them actors. Well, "extras" now have to be called "SAs" – Supporting Artistes. It's a bit like football. Linesmen now have to be called "referee's assistants". The world has gone barmy and the moon is made of cheese!

We had a lot of fun making *ChuckleVision*. We had basic scripts to work from but we ad-libbed quite a lot as well. That is one of the big advantages that Barry and I had and especially since we had our older brothers along as well. We all know each other inside out and one has only to mention a word and we are immediately on the same wavelength and can see the gag through.

Sometimes the visual gags would go wrong and a pretend bang on the head would end up being a real one. Whoever it was would be holding their head in their hands while the rest of us could not stop laughing. It's a cruel world, isn't it?

We had some great props in *ChuckleVision* as well and some marvellous locations and sets. I loved a couple of episodes we did with ice cream vans. It took me back to my time as an ice cream salesman and, let's be honest, I have always enjoyed ice cream so between shoots I was the ice cream van's best customer.

Talking of SAs, we did have some great people to work with, although sometimes it took quite a few takes to actually get a scene exactly as we wanted. I remember one scene in a hospital. I was supposed to be a patient on a trolley with Barry pushing me. Barry had to sprint down this corridor with the trolley travelling like a sports car and me clinging on. A lady who, with respect, was past middle-age was supposed to be sitting on a bench in the corridor and had to watch as we flew past.

All she had to do was turn her head in surprise as the trolley went flying past her. You would not think that it would be such a problem but she just could not get the timing right. She would look too soon, too late, too slowly, too quick. You name it, she did everything except get it right. We did take after take. Barry was getting totally knackered by having to keep sprinting up and down this corridor pushing the trolley and I was starting to get travel sick! We got there in the end but we lost count of how many takes it had taken – and how much time as well.

If you have seen the show you will also have seen the outtakes at the end. They are quite genuine and sometimes more funny than the actual gag. The trouble is that once you find something funny it is difficult to get it right. Barry and I are terrible for collapsing with laughter when something has gone wrong and the trouble is that when we try again we only have to look at each other for the fits of laughter to start again.

The most common mistake is to forget someone's name or a complete line but there is also a problem with spoonerisms and sometimes they can be hilarious and on the odd occasion, something is said that you definitely could not show as an outtake.

I love it when someone else gets something wrong and I have to resist making it worse. Sometimes the other person in a scene has taken a few minutes out to get a grip on themselves and finally they steel themselves to have another go at the scene. When they face me I like to just smile a very little and raise one eyebrow and that usually starts them off again. I then look innocently at the director and shrug my shoulders.

The scripts were mostly written by John Sayle, Barry and myself although we also had Russell T. Davis on board for some of them, which was great because Russell is best known for his work on *Dr Who* and is a brilliant writer.

ChuckleVision has been fantastic for us and we have been grateful for what it has done for two lads from Rotherham who didn't fancy going into the steel or coal industries.

Chapter 13

TV and Tours

A lot of people ask if *ChuckleVision* will be back on our screens and we simply don't know. There is a petition going to bring us back and thousands of people have already signed so anything might yet happen. The younger generation is always changing so perhaps the BBC will decide to start showing our repeats once again.

There is not much we can do about it except hope that fan power might work. The BBC tend to listen to viewers rather than people like us. We would like to do more of course and there are still plenty of ideas, so who knows?

In the meantime we keep busy with pantos and tours. This year we were back in Darlington at the Civic Theatre for the 2104 panto and it was great fun again.

We do love the live shows, whether our touring shows or panto, and have been on the road with the Chuckle Brothers stage shows for quite some time now. We pick a different theme every year and have been pirates, spacemen, adventurers, all sorts of things. It is like doing panto but on an even bigger scale.

We have been on desert islands, in haunted castles and even on a different planet, something which many will say we have been on for a long, long time.

The sets and all the equipment get to the theatre about nine o'clock in the morning and the crew dress the stage, sort out the lighting and the sound and get everything ready until we arrive. We travel together and often play cards on the way in the back of our camper. We actually run a league with points for every game you win. We never, ever play for money, this is just for fun.

I usually top the cards league of course because I am the best at playing cards, just as I am the best at golf. Barry says I am also the best at talking about it. I'm not sure what he means by that!

We don't always play cards, sometimes we just relax and Barry will read a paper or something while I have a go on my Playstation. I love those games. I like the ones that test your mental skills as well as your finger skills. I'm not into the violent stuff, just a bit of football or some other challenge.

When we get to the theatre we usually find that everything is ready for us and that our guests, most often Safire, are already there and have set up their stuff as well. We do a bit of a sound check and then relax before the show.

There is a really great feeling when you arrive at a theatre and they tell you that the show has already sold out. That has happened quite a lot of times and it really gives you a lift because you know you are going to have a fantastic time on stage and that you have a really big and probably noisy audience to have fun with.

After each show we go to an arranged spot and sit and sign autographs, meet people and have our photos taken with them. Quite often we meet the same people over and over again and they will bring us photos of their kids taken with us the year before or even a few years before so that we can see how they have grown.

Barry and I actually like that. We always feel as if we are meeting up with old friends and when we see their children growing up it is like sharing time with some of the family. So keep coming to see us and keep bringing us your photos to see.

We get stopped quite a lot in the street too and at restaurants and in hotels and shops. We must be easily recognised because we are often asked to pose with someone for a photo and they tell us they used to watch us when they were little. Since some of them are now in their twenties that's a bit of a worry! I pretend I haven't heard that bit and pretend they have said that they have just started watching us on TV. I'm too young to start getting old!

For the last few years we have not taken a long summer season in one place but travelled from theatre to theatre with our Chuckle Brothers show. We have a tour organised for us and during the main six weeks of the summer we might be in Skegness every Tuesday, Great Yarmouth every Wednesday and so on. That's quite good in some senses because that way you get to know where the best chip shops are.

We try to get a holiday between the end of the summer season and the start of rehearsals for panto but we also get involved with filming for other television shows. Once the panto season ends we grab our main holiday before starting with the spring tour which usually begins a little before Easter.

We decide what the theme of the tour will be during the summer of the year before so that there is plenty of time for scripting, scenery making and all the other ingredients that go into making a show that we will be happy with.

Giving a really good, value-for-money show is very, very important to both of us. We would hate to think that anyone might go home disappointed. Perhaps that's why we try to spray as many people with our water pistols as we possibly can. We wouldn't want anyone to feel left out!!

Being the Chuckle Brothers has other benefits too. We have often been invited to appear on other shows, we often get to sit in the directors' box at football matches and we get to meet all sorts of famous people, including the Royal Family. That is always a thrill because they are very special people and I don't think we always appreciate how much the rest of the world envies us for our great history and our Royal Family.

I remember talking to Princess Anne once and telling her about the time we met her Auntie. She really laughed because not many people have called Princess Margaret "Auntie". We met both of them in connection with charities and that is another big bonus when you become a little bit of a celebrity. Both Barry and I have always tried to do our best to help different charities. I'm not going to go into details because that would sound wrong but if I tell you that for the privileged to be able to help the under-privileged carries with it a great personal reward, you will know how we feel about it.

So where we do go from here? Well, the touring show will go on rolling for some time to come. We have lots of themes up our sleeves and we just love doing those shows, so as long as people want to see the shows we shall keep going with them.

The same applies to pantomimes. We love panto, we love all the fun, the noise, the singing and the general mayhem that goes on. It can be hard work but it is you, the audience, who carry us along and make the hard work really worth it. An audience that is enjoying itself gives life and energy to performers so we'll keep going if you will... please!

We have some ideas being considered for more television shows and we have a few other irons in the fire so it looks as if the Chuckle Brothers are going to be around for some time yet. Both Barry and I certainly hope so.

Chapter 14

Magic Moments

Everybody has their favourite moments in life and it is fair to say that Barry and I have had more than our fair share. Yes, of course, we have had our disappointments, some of them really bad and we have had some dreadful emotional lows with bereavements and so on which makes us all the more determined to make people laugh and try to relieve some of the sadness that grips us all from time to time.

Your Magic Moments usually start when you are a kid and I have already talked about Barry and I growing up together but there are still some other things that you cherish even though they only come back to you now and then.

As an example, we used to love the radio and on Sundays we especially loved listening to the *Billy Cotton Band Show* around lunchtime. What a great performer, a real showman. We loved every minute of it from the moment he yelled into the microphone: "Wakey! Wakey!"

We also loved *Educating Archie*, which was another Sunday lunchtime show. When you really think about, how on earth did they get away with having a radio show starring a ventriloquist and his doll? They did though and Archie Andrews became an international star, travelling the world with Peter Brough. He was especially popular in Australia I am told. I have also heard a rumour that Archie Andrews might be making a comeback though I don't know if that's likely to be on radio or in theatres.

Having said that, we also liked *Worker's Playtime* and as well as singers and comedians, that show also included magicians. Yes, a radio show with magicians! You could never see how they did the tricks!

Are you ready for a confession? One of the radio Magic Moments for Barry and I was listening to the Ovaltinies. It was always very cosy listening to the radio, especially at Sunday lunchtimes because of the smell of roast dinner, the warmth of the room and the fun we had as a family gathered round to listen was something very special and a happy memory for all of us.

Of course there was a big occasion when our first television arrived. We were totally hypnotised even before the delivery man plugged it in. This new piece of furniture was like a window on the world. It was modern and most people still didn't have one so we had not seen much of it elsewhere. It is amazing how such a thing could become such an adventure, but it was.

The television consisted of a great big, shining cabinet with a nine inch screen. Nowadays if you had a screen that small you would watch it through binoculars because we are used to having screens big enough to rival the local cinema. In those days of the 1950s though the nine inch screen was a magical piece of luxury and we were thrilled with it.

Yes, okay, time for another confession. Barry and I used to

watch *Andy Pandy*. We also watched *Bill and Ben the Flower Pot Men* and that very annoying Weed. If they ever do a remake they should audition Barry to be the Weed. He would be perfect. He's got the build for it – and he's naturally annoying!

We liked *Muffin the Mule* as well and one of our really huge favourites was *Mr Pastry*. What a brilliant slapstick star he was, or rather Richard Hearn who created the character of Mr Pastry.

On Coronation Day in 1953 we were involved in the street party. I carried the crown around our street and the neighbouring street on a purple cushion, leading the parade. It wasn't the real crown of course and the cushion wasn't quite the right purple but it did match the curtains at No 17 and for me it was a solemn occasion and a great honour to carry the "crown". We still had time to watch the Coronation on television though and in almost every street in the land there was one house, or possibly two, that had about eighty people packed into its sitting room as they were the only people in the street with a television!

Happy days and Magic Moments as we were growing up!

We have had some great highs as well as the lows and hopefully this book will have helped us share them with you. When we got our first paid engagement in show business we really were "over the moon". Getting the gig is very often more exciting than actually fulfilling it as your nerves start jangling when you arrive at the venue and you start asking yourself questions like: "What am I doing here?" or "Am I really cut out for this?" with of course "What if they hate us? Will we get out alive?!"

Barry had a bit of an advantage over me because he had already been doing gigs playing drums, but appearing as a double act trying to make people laugh was very different.

We knew more than most newcomers because of our Dad and our brothers but when you go on that stage for the first time in your own right it is a scary experience so, as I said, getting confirmation of the gig is the more exciting part of the whole thing.

Getting a summer season was also a big thrill. It might have been in a holiday camp with lots of extra jobs to do but when we heard that we had got the booking we could not have been more pleased if you had told us we were to top the bill for a season at the London Palladium.

Getting the thumbs up for *Opportunity Knocks* was also a massive thrill. Television was very special in those days and not everyone got the chance. Television is still great in many ways but with so many channels now and so many "reality" shows plus lots of shows about cooking, houses, travel, keeping streets clean, running guests houses and so on, it seems as if just about everyone will get their five minutes of fame. Still, we were lucky, we managed to get on television when there were not so many options and chances so we were always grateful for that and loved every minute of it.

Getting our own television show with *ChuckleVision* was another very special moment and when it was finally broadcast on September 20th, 1987 and family and friends – including the neighbours – started to tell us that they had watched the show and really enjoyed it, we were thrilled all over again. Those are real Magic Moments.

There have been others though and I never realised this before but you have to be careful what you say and how you say it because you can come over as smug or big-headed and I should hate that to come across because we are not at all like that. We are very grateful for what success we have had and most especially to those who have watched out TV shows, come to see us at the theatre and given us a friendly wave when we have been seen walking along the street. Some of you may be reading this so a really big thanks from both Barry and I, we are very, very grateful for all you have done for us.

Nevertheless, you can't help enjoying some of the privileges that come your way when you have had a bit of success, especially in show business. I know that I have had the chance to play on some great golf courses because of being one of the Chuckle Brothers and there have been some Magic Moments on the greens – some pretty awful moments too! We won't talk about those, though.

Probably one of the most special of our Magic Moments – perhaps THE most special – happened a few years ago when we were at Basingstoke, appearing at the Anvil, a really nice modern theatre. A lady came to see us with her little girl and told us her story, a tale which quite honestly had both Barry and myself in tears in the dressing room afterwards.

The little girl had been in an accident and had gone into a coma. It was only a life-support machine that kept her going and there was not much hope that she would survive but her mother did not give up on trying to find something that would help her little girl.

The doctors told the mother the sad news that if her daughter did not revive by the Monday they would have to switch off the life-support machine. She was told that on the Friday. At home later that day *ChuckleVision* was on TV and she knew that her daughter would have been glued to it. She quickly recorded the theme music on a cassette and took it to the hospital the next day.

She switched on the tape and let it play. After about thirty seconds a smile spread across her daughter's face and she said: "Is it on Mum?"

We had the great privilege of meeting that little girl after she had recovered.

I can still feel the tears as I relate that story. To think we had played a part in saving a lovely little girl's life is just fantastic. You don't get more magical moments than that.

Whenever we get invited to a children's hospital we simply can't say "no". We just couldn't do that, especially at Christmastime when some kids are in hospital. It is so sad for them even though the hospitals and the staff do their best to make it okay for them. For us, to go along and to make them laugh or giggle when they're not feeling well is very heart-warming. Nowadays when we go in to see them it's usually the mum and dads that are gobsmacked at seeing us and wanting to have their photos taken with us!

A favourite charity of ours is a charity called PACT. If I've got it right it stands for Parents and Children with Trauma. The hospital is Sheffield Children's Hospital and what they do is buy properties close to the hospital for parents to stay in when their child is hospitalised. Such a great thing, especially when the family travel from as far as the likes of Lincoln. The hardship on the family is massive. It's such a help for them to have somewhere to sleep close to their child, so we do our best to be supportive of them.

As well as these great privileges, another of the benefits of being in this business is that you get to meet some great people too, either because you work with them, meet them at some reception or other, or you are sent tickets to go and see them in their own shows.

Ken Dodd is one of those. It has been a privilege to meet him and to see him at work. He is a legend, of course, and you have to see at least one of his shows to really appreciate his brilliance. I don't know how he does it but to keep up a performance like that when you are in the latter half of your eighties is just totally amazing and sets him apart from all others.

I can recall two regular Magic Moments with Doddy – seeing the reaction from the audience when he first appears on stage and then hearing the audience showing their appreciation hours later as he takes his bow at the end of the show.

You might not think that people who earn a living through comedy don't want to see other comics or comedy shows but Barry and I have always been fans of comedy as well as taking part in it. Watching the great Tommy Cooper at the Fiesta Club in Stockton was an eye-opener. He was such a funny guy. When I tell you he was announced onto the stage and the roar of cheers and adoration was deafening. His intro music was playing but the tabs (curtains, sorry, habit calling curtains tabs) were still closed and after what seemed like five minutes at least, the audience slowly calmed down to an almost hush. No sign on stage of anyone, then came the wonderful sound of "huh huh huh" from the man. That's all it needed to get one of the biggest laughs we've heard from an opener.

For the next five minutes he did stupid trick after stupid trick and his usual one liners – and the curtains still hadn't opened! Eventually, after saying things like "there's not many in tonight" the tabs opened and he was facing the band at the back of the stage. Absolute roars of laughter! He would always think "out of the box", Tommy, and we definitely learned a lot watching him. Visual comedy is everlasting.

Frankie Howard was another great comic who had to be seen live to fully appreciate how good he really was. Most people only ever saw him on television or in his various movies but I'm telling you he was another genius.

It speaks volumes that these great legends of comedy never had to go on stage and use four-letter words. We still don't fully understand what that is all about. There are some great comics in show business today but however funny they are, some make themselves unfit for family viewing and it's a great shame because many of them are genuinely funny guys.

When you have some success on television people start coming up with other ideas and suggestions for you and that is always a bit of a Magic Moment because it is nice to be thought of, even if you don't actually like the idea. Every now and then someone comes with an idea that makes you think it is worth a try and that is how it was for our game show, which ran for a couple of years from 1996 to 1998 and was called *To Me... To You!* I wonder where that title came from?

Actually that catchphrase was not invented for our shows, it was something we used to say when we were kids growing up in Rotherham. If Mum or Dad asked us to move a chair or something we would do it between us and give each other instructions, so "To Me... To You" was born all those years ago when we were just kids.

Anyway, in the show we were on a kind of Treasure Island and the children contestants had to do different games to help them win a bamboo truck full of prizes. The bamboo truck was actually a disguised shopping trolley – but you couldn't have a shopping trolley on a desert island. The trolley was on wheels on a rail track which ran in a semi circle and the idea was to get your trolley TO ME at the end of the rail to win the prizes on the trolley. The dice had numbers TO YOU 3 (or 2 etc.) and TO ME 3 (likewise).

The kids arrived at the island at the start of the show by ferry. Our favourite game was down at the swamp. Each week we had guest stars arrive too. Among them were Kieran Bracken, the England Rugby Union captain, athletics star Kelly Holmes, two members of STEPS – who were massive at that time – and even the most well known of all weather men (can't remember his name now!).

Just kidding, he was Michael Fish, who was famous for saying there will be a bit of a blow this weekend but nothing to worry about (or words to the like). What happened? We had hurricane-style winds and the worst storms across the South, storms that still hold records. So much for "a bit of a blow but nothing to worry about"!

We did three series of that show and it went well but to be honest it was all getting a bit too much for us and we were getting totally kn... tired so we decided to shelve it for some possible future use. We have never taken it up again but possibly that was a mistake because we did enjoy the show very much.

In 2008, the BBC broadcast a documentary series called *Comedy Map of Britain* and it featured many of the big names of British comedy. We had another Magic Moment when we were asked to feature in the series. To find yourselves being mentioned in the same programme as so many comedy greats is quite a humbling experience. Imagine that – Norman Wisdom, Les Dawson, Ken Dodd, Tommy Cooper, Max Miller, Arthur Askey, the Crazy Gang and the Chuckle Brothers. Wow!

We had another Magic Moment in 2010 when we won a special award. No, it wasn't an Oscar – it was a TV series called *Celebrity Coach Trip*. Nothing but the best for us! Actually it was a bit of fun, a little like I'm a *Celebrity Get Me Out of Here* but without eating maggots and living in an exotic location.

Barry and I were well used to spending time on a coach – remember all those coach trips to Cleethorpes when we were kids – so we probably had a head start over everyone else. Anyway, we lasted the whole journey and were declared the winners. I'm not actually sure what we won but it was still a fun gig.

There was talk of us going on *I'm a Celebrity Get Me Out of Here* but it hasn't actually happened yet. We would love to go to Australia of course, especially if it was to present our own stage show and see something of the country and we would certainly be pleased to be asked to have a go at I'm a Celebrity. If we were and we did, I wonder if they would let us take Ray Mears with us to help us survive!

Barry had a special moment all on his own for Christmas 2013. We have always enjoyed shows like *Only Fools and Horses, Porridge* and *Open All Hours* and when they decided to do a Christmas special called *Still Open All Hours* with David Jason now running the shop, Barry was asked to appear as Mr Marshall, a slightly eccentric dog owner. Barry was thrilled to appear in one of his all-time favourite TV comedy shows. Me? I offered to play the dog but they said they already had a comedy lead. Sorry about that, but it was the best I could come up with!

Talking of David Jason, both Barry and I have been big fans of his for a long time. At the end of our stage shows – for those who have never been to one – we come out and meet the audience afterwards. They queue up and we sit at a table and sign autographs for them, have a little chat and pose for photos with them. Can you imagine how stunned we were when we looked up at the next person in the queue and came face to face with David Jason and his daughter? They had been to see the show and then queued for our autographs. Imagine that – our hero, David Jason, queuing up to get our autographs! What a Magic Moment that was.

Jonathon Ross also came to see us with his family and we were told that at one performance we did at a theatre in Kent – Maidstone I think it was – Elton quietly slipped in to see the show. Understandably he didn't join the queue for an autograph afterwards, but we hope he enjoyed the show.

Our fans and friends are totally amazing. There is one chap who has his entire room decorated with Chuckle Brothers posters, photos and other souvenirs. Amazing! Our fans have also been campaigning to get *ChuckleVision* back on BBC TV. That's really nice of them. One even told the papers that today's children are missing out by not being able to watch a dose of the Chuckle Brothers every day. That makes us sound like a foul-tasting medicine, but we appreciate the thought!

One thing we have always had trouble with is using the word "fans". It doesn't sound quite right to us because it always sounds a bit like 'them and us'. We don't see it that way. We always consider that our viewers and our live audiences are part of the show. We are in it together. When we come off the stage with water pistols and start firing them at the audience, they are certainly part of the show then!

The trouble is if we call you all followers it sounds like we have become a religion and if we call you supporters we sound like a football team so we'll have to settle for fans – but think of it more as friends.

Another thing that is always special for us is being able to help charities, especially children's charities. It is sad that there is never enough time to be able to say "yes" to everything we are asked to do but we do our best and have had some fun with *Comic Relief* and other charity shows both on TV and at theatres. There is something special about being able to do something to help those less fortunate than yourself and when it is for children that makes it all the better. There is nothing so special as seeing a child smile or, even better, to hear them laugh and when those kids are laughing through some pretty awful circumstances your heart goes out to them. That is when being famous is really worthwhile because you can make a difference, just a little bit anyway.

I can honestly tell you that we always get a real thrill when we are asked to open something. We are just ordinary lads really so when we are asked to be special guests at something or to cut the ribbon somewhere it is always a bit special. As with the charities, we often have to say sorry that we just can't fit it in, but we do try our best to accept invitations.

One we really enjoyed was opening the new lemur enclose at the Tropical Butterfly House, Wildlife and Falconry Centre in North Anston. Both Barry and I have always liked and taken an interest in animals, which is one of the reasons we enjoyed working in circuses so much.

Actually, working in the circus gives you a great sense of family as circus folk are the salt of the earth. Great people. Norman Barrett was ringmaster at Blackpool Tower Circus for many years and it's his fault that we tend to shake hands with people we work with on a daily basis. He told us on about day three of rehearsals in 1974 that every day we came in he would shake our hands. We had not encountered this before of course, so we wanted to know why. It seemed odd to us. Normally anyone would say "nice to meet you" or whatever and shake hands, but when you'd only seen them the day before you don't expect it.

Norman never did actually explain it but as the days turned into weeks we noticed that everyone who works in circus does shake hands with everybody else every day. Strange, I know, but it soon becomes a natural thing to do. It is not just the custom in Britain either. Wherever you go in the world, circus folk greet each other – even close friends who have their caravans parked next to each other – with a handshake.

As I was saying, working in circus is – or was – a great thing to be able to get that close up to the animals, which, may I tell you, were looked after better than we were! To feel the coat of a snow leopard will live with me forever and to touch a lion or an elephant is something very special. Believe it or not the only thing we were told not to go near were the sea lions. We were told not to get too close as they have a very nasty bite on them. I did suggest to Barry that he might like to find out if that was true, but he didn't. He always was a bit of a cowardy custard. I wouldn't mind, but I had some plasters with me just in case.

So, with that in mind, being asked to open a wildlife centre was brilliant. The birds of prey were fantastic. One of them had his eye on Barry and I am sure he thought he was a bone with just a bit of meat on!

Another Magic Moment for me was riding a motorbike during a great holiday on the beautiful Greek island of Cephalonia. I have always been a car person really because I would sooner have a roof over my head when it's raining, but I have also quite liked motorbikes and I couldn't resist hiring one while on holiday.

The clear blue skies told me that there was no chance of rain but they didn't tell me about the herds of goats that are walked along the roads of Cephalonia. I met one unexpectedly and in a bid to avoid a collision I went one way and the motorbike went another way. I ended up on the ground with a broken nose, cuts and bruises and a group of untouched goats staring at me in disbelief.

That was not the worst of it because as I got my senses back I became aware of a group of people looking around for the TV cameras. They recognised me and thought we were filming for one of our shows. One of them even called out "To me... to you!" They didn't rush to help me in case it spoiled the filming!

A few years ago one of the young men's magazines started a campaign to get us knighted. It was a really nice idea and we appreciated the thought but it would never have really happened. Can you imagine Her Majesty saying "Arise Sir Chuckle" without bursting into laughter. Still, Barry has the OBEM – One Born Every Minute!

Not all of our moments have been magic as you will have gathered by now and there is one thing that we have found quite upsetting. On more than one occasion someone has started a rumour that Barry has had a heart attack and died.

That is a pretty dreadful thing to say, even as a joke. We like to think that we have a pretty good sense of humour but that has not even raised a smile. Even putting aside the stress caused to Barry and his family, there are children everywhere who love our shows and come to see us regularly. They see us as good and funny friends, they write to us, they have their photos taken with us after the shows and we have become part of their family. For them to be reduced to tears because some idiot thinks it's funny to say that one of us has died, is quite unforgivable.

Let's change the subject and go back to a real Magic Moment in 2008 when we received the Special Award at the Children's BAFTA Awards. Awards are like cream cakes. You go into a room and see them and you want one but you assume they are for other people so you pretend not to notice them. We never expected to get any sort of award but it was great when it happened.

It was presented to us by Russell T. Davies who has written many of the Doctor Who scripts and also wrote a couple of episodes of *ChuckleVision* in his early days of writing. That's why he was asked to present us with our BAFTA.

Receiving the award was such a great moment, a Magic Moment in fact. Unusually they gave us one each and we were very thankful for that as Barry wouldn't have been happy going home without one. Keith Chegwin hosted the awards ceremony and told everyone we were "bloomin' fantastic" which is exactly how we felt about the award.

One Magic Moment we are still looking forward to is being there at Wembley when Rotherham United win the FA Cup! We have never swayed from supporting Rotherham, although I also have a soft spot for Liverpool. We always give Rotherham a mention on both *ChuckleVision* and our stage shows and have been huge fans since we were kids. You can imagine how we felt when the then club chairman Denis Coleman made us honorary members of the club in 2007. That was just fantastic and we still go to as many games as possible.

I hope you don't mind but I would like to take this moment to say a huge "thank you" to our current chairman Tony Stewart, without whom our beloved team might have gone out of existence. He also has a twin brother, Terry, whose job it was to travel all over the country looking at stadiums to see which style would be best for the Millers. I reckon he deserves a knighthood for bringing New York Stadium to Rotherham. Well, thank you Tony and Terry for that. It is a superb stadium and you have done us proud.

So, with a new stadium and great results, the Millers are on their way to the Premiership and maybe even to Europe. Now wouldn't that be a Magic Moment!

We are lucky in that most people love to hear laughter, especially the laughter of children and we hear that all the time. We are basically clowns who make people laugh for a living. Sometimes when we do an interview with the papers or others people try to analyse it or turn it into some great psychological phenomenon. There, you didn't know I could use long words like that, did you? Don't ask me to repeat it, I'll never get it right twice.

Laughter is a kind of magic that says so much and does so

much good. Comedy goes back as far as humankind and our kind of comedy has been there from the start. If someone trips over, bangs into a post, hits their thumb with a hammer, speaks funny or says the wrong thing without giving offence, everyone else finds it funny.

You cannot instruct people to find something funny. Sometimes people try but it never lasts very long. Least of all you cannot tell kids what they must laugh at. They will tell you if it is funny or not and there is nothing better than to hear them when they do laugh at something you do or say.

We keep trying new things, new gags, new ideas, new themes for our shows both on stage and for television because we feel we owe it to ourselves and to our audiences to give them something fresh to enjoy, but the basic ingredient is slapstick whether it is physical or spoken. If it's funny, it's funny.

I could go on and on but maybe I'll save all that for when we do another book in 2064. In the meantime, thanks to everyone for making our moments so magical and we hope that in return you will all have a special Magic Moment of your own – the day you saw the Chuckle Brothers!

We have had a ball and we hope you have too, so let's keep on doing it. After all, life would not be the same if Barry and I could not look at each other and say "To Me… To You."